HEALTH REPORTS:
DISEASES AND DISORDERS

LUPUS

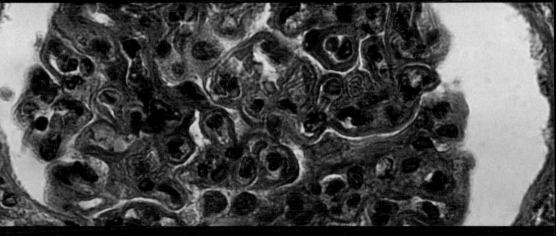

KARIN RHINES

TWENTY-FIRST CENTURY BOOKS
MINNEAPOLIS

Twenty-First Century Books
A division of Lerner Publishing Group, Inc.
241 First Avenue North
Minneapolis, MN 55401 U.S.A.

Website address: www.lernerbooks.com

Library of Congress Cataloging-in-Publication Data

Rhines, Karin.
    Lupus / by Karin Rhines.
        p.   cm.—(USA TODAY health reports: diseases and disorders)
    Includes bibliographical references and index.
    ISBN 978-0-8225-8582-4 (lib. bdg. : alk. paper)
    1. Systemic lupus erythematosus—Juvenile literature. I. Title.
RC924.5.L85R55 2012
616.7'72—dc22   2009020582

Manufactured in the United States of America
1 – DP – 12/31/11

CONTENTS

USA TODAY
HEALTH REPORTS:
DISEASES AND DISORDERS

CHAPTER ONE

LUPUS: THE GREAT IMITATOR

NATALIE

Natalie flinched when her fingers hit the computer keyboard. She was having one of her bad days. When she awoke that morning, the joints in her fingers and wrists had hurt. And the pain had gotten worse as the day progressed. Natalie works as a paralegal and uses a computer a lot. She plans to go to law school as soon as her husband finishes his master's degree. But if this thing with her hands keeps getting worse, she's not sure she'll be able to. She has seen two doctors, but they've just told her to take aspirin. Natalie thought she might have arthritis, but her grandmother said that twenty-eight was too young for that. Natalie hoped she was right as she watched her grandmother struggle to use her crippled hands.

CHARLES

Charles, known as Dunk to his friends, lay on the bed in his room, mostly ignoring the sports news on TV. The walls were lined with pictures of him playing basketball. A first-place trophy from the statewide championships sat on a bookcase. But on this day, he was so tired that he couldn't even enjoy his favorite sportscaster. He didn't much care about the highlights of his favorite team. He just wanted to sleep, even though it was only seven in the evening. He was tired and tired of feeling tired. He'd been having days like this since his senior year in high school. At first it was once or twice a month, but now it was almost every week. He kept thinking that a twenty-year-old shouldn't feel like this. He should be able to work with his uncle's painting company *all day and then shoot hoops and party with his friends every night. But his life wasn't working out that way.*

JASMINE

Jasmine yawned and rubbed her eyes. She didn't like mornings, especially when they started this early. She had band practice before classes. She wanted to do well in band, so she could meet her goal of being the first-chair trombone player in ninth grade the following year. She thought it would be so cool for a girl to play first trombone. Jasmine was eating her cereal when her mother startled her by asking, "How did you get that sunburn? Haven't you been using your sunscreen?" She reminded her mother that it had been raining for two days. Then she caught her reflection in the toaster on the counter. She had big red splotches on both cheeks and across her nose. It was ugly! Her mother looked more closely at Jasmine's face and then put the back of her hand to Jasmine's forehead. "You're hot," she said, "no school today." Jasmine started to protest, but the look on her mother's face told her that there was no use arguing.

Lupus can cause extreme fatigue in some people, causing them to fall asleep during the day and miss their regular activities.

Natalie, Charles, and Jasmine may not seem to have anything in common, but they do. They all have lupus, but they don't know it yet.

Of the people who have heard of lupus, many have mistaken ideas about it. Lupus is often called the great imitator because it appears in different ways in different people. It can appear as fatigue in one person or joint aches in another or rashes, fever, or headaches. None of these symptoms seem especially threatening alone, but they can signal lupus, a potentially life-threatening disease.

WHAT IS LUPUS?

Lupus occurs when the immune system malfunctions. Normally the immune system defends the body from diseases caused by microorganisms such as bacteria, viruses, and parasites. It creates chemicals called antibodies to fight invaders. But in people with lupus, the antibodies turn on the body and cause the symptoms already mentioned. In severe cases, lupus can also affect the heart, lungs, the nervous system, and especially the kidneys. In some cases, lupus causes death. Lupus is not contagious (one

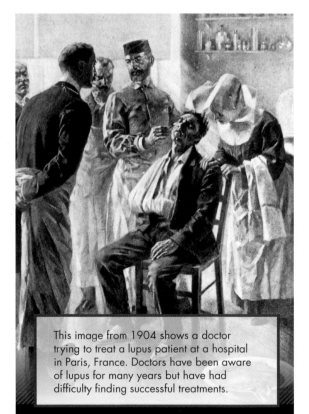

This image from 1904 shows a doctor trying to treat a lupus patient at a hospital in Paris, France. Doctors have been aware of lupus for many years but have had difficulty finding successful treatments.

person cannot give it to another). But it is chronic—so once you have lupus, it doesn't go away.

Lupus is not a new disease. Medical writings from two thousand years ago describe the lupus rash. The illness characterized by a rash across the nose and cheeks was named *lupus erythematosus* in the mid-1800s. *Lupus* means "wolf" in Latin, and the pattern of the rash, sometimes called a butterfly rash, was thought to resemble the mask of a wolf. The term *erythematosus*, from the Greek word for "redden," refers to the red color of the rash. Physicians identified other symptoms in the early twentieth century. They learned that this illness affected many different body systems other than the skin. The name *systemic lupus erythematosus*, or SLE, reflects that lupus affects the whole body. Researchers developed the first blood test to help diagnose lupus in the 1950s.

WHO GETS LUPUS?

Between one million and two million people in the United States are thought to have lupus. But the real number may be much higher because diagnosis can be difficult. Like many diseases, lupus does not strike everyone equally. Most cases of SLE (80 to 90 percent) are seen in women between the ages of sixteen and forty-four. But both men and women of any age can have lupus. Lupus can occur in children, but this is uncommon. Children and men tend to have more serious forms of lupus. People who develop the disease after the age of sixty tend to have milder forms. Women who are diagnosed during their childbearing years generally have milder symptoms after menopause, the time when the ovaries stop functioning. People of any race or ethnicity can get lupus. But in the United States, more African Americans, Hispanics, Asians, and American Indians have lupus than Caucasians.

Studying Lupus and Ethnicity

I n 1993 a long-term research project call LUMINA (Lupus in Minorities: Nature versus Nurture) began. Its purpose is to find out how lupus affects different ethnic groups. The study began with 229 African American, Hispanic, and Caucasian women from Texas and Puerto Rico who had had lupus for five years or less. Researchers determined ethnicity by the women's grandparents (all four had to be of the same ethnicity). These women underwent testing and shared their medical records when the study began. Since then, they have met with researchers each year for follow-ups.

The study has found that African American and Hispanic women have more serious lupus when they are diagnosed than Caucasians do. Kidney damage caused by lupus is often the symptom that leads to the diagnosis. In addition, African American women often have scarring from lupus-caused skin damage. The reason for this difference is not yet clear, but many African American women are poor. Poverty often goes hand in hand with lack of access to medical care.

As the study continues, new recruits replace women who have dropped out of the study. The study is looking at ways that genetics interact with social, psychological, and economic factors in the lives of these women.

WHAT CAUSES LUPUS?

Physicians have known about lupus for well over one hundred years, but they still do not know the cause. Several factors probably interact to cause lupus. Researchers are studying genetics, hormones, environment, and stress as possible causes. *Genetics* is the study of how characteristics are passed down, or inherited, from one generation to the next. It is not unusual to find two or more members of a family with lupus. To try to identify the role of genes in lupus, researchers have studied twins. Twins are favorite subjects for research into the influence of genetics on disease. There are two types of twins: fraternal and identical. Fraternal twins come from two separate eggs fertilized by two different sperm. Genetically, fraternal twins are no more alike than any other two siblings. They just happen to have been born at the same time. Identical twins, on the other hand, come from a single fertilized egg and are genetically identical, which is why they look alike. If a disease is caused by genes,

Doctors and researchers hope that genetics research will help them better understand the causes of lupus and will lead to better treatments.

both fraternal twins in a pair should be no more likely to have the disease than any other pair of siblings. With identical twins, if one twin has a disease caused by genes, the other should have it as well.

Studies have shown that if one fraternal twin has lupus, the other has about a 2 percent chance of having the disease. This is also the case for siblings who are not twins. In identical twins, if one twin has lupus, the other twin has a 20 percent chance of having lupus. This finding supports the idea that genes are involved in lupus. In fact, more than a dozen genes may play a role in lupus. However, since there is only a 20 percent chance that both identical twins will have lupus, genes cannot be the whole explanation.

Hormones are another factor under study. The individuals most likely to have lupus are women between the ages of sixteen and forty-four, the years when female hormones are at their peak. It seems like an obvious connection, and in mice it is. Researchers have found that removing the female hormone estrogen or giving the male hormone testosterone stops lupus in mice. Similar research on humans has not provided a clear answer. Hormone research also does not explain lupus in men of all ages or in older women, all of whom have lower levels of female hormones. Female hormones most likely have a role in lupus, but they are not the only trigger.

An individual's environment, including pollution, toxins (poisons), and infections, may be connected to lupus. No specific pollutant or toxin has yet been linked to the disease. But infection, especially infection by viruses, may hold another key. The immune system can usually defeat viral infections, but sometimes viruses can remain hidden in the body and set the stage for or even trigger lupus at some later time. The Epstein-Barr virus, which causes infectious mononucleosis, seems to have a link to lupus.

Researchers are investigating the role of stress in lupus. Stress, especially ongoing, low-level stress, can have a dramatic effect on the body and the immune system. Fear of being bullied or worry about doing well in school can cause low-level stress. Stress may be the final straw for people who already have genes that make them susceptible to lupus and a virus lurking in their bodies.

HOW IS LUPUS TREATED?

A person with lupus needs to be under a doctor's care. In severe cases of lupus, where body organs are affected, a whole team of doctors may be involved. Rheumatologists, doctors who specialize in treating diseases of the joints, muscles, and bones, play an important role in diagnosing and treating lupus because malfunctions of the immune system can cause damage to joints, muscles, and bones. If the illness involves internal organs, nephrologists (kidney specialists), cardiologists (heart specialists), neurologists (nervous system specialists), or pulmonologists (lung specialists) will be part of the team.

Medications can treat the symptoms, but there is no magic bullet, no single drug, and no cure. In the mid-1900s, half of the people with lupus died within four years of their diagnosis. In the twenty-first century, because of treatment advances, most people with lupus can live normal, active lives. In fact, people whose lupus does not involve internal organs often have a normal life span. Those with severe lupus, however, may find that the illness restricts their activities. If these individuals cannot get the specialized treatment they need or if their treatment does not work, they will die young.

MORTALITY

The leading causes of death related to lupus are kidney disease, infections, and disease of the heart and blood vessels. Mortality rates

Journalist and Storyteller with Lupus

Charles Kuralt was a war correspondent during the Vietnam War 1957–1975) and a television news reporter. He won Peabody and Emmy awards for his journalism and wrote six books. He was best known for his "On the Road" TV features. He crisscrossed the United States, traveling 50,000 miles (80,467 kilometers) a year. He visited small towns and out-of-the-way places. He was pudgy and balding and had an easy way with people. He made more than six hundred episodes of "On the Road." Some were interviews of ordinary people with interesting stories. Others were his reflections on the wonders of the U.S. landscape. In 1997, at the age of sixty-two, he died from complications of lupus.

Charles Kuralt, shown here in 1991, died of complications of lupus in 1997.

(number of deaths for each one hundred thousand people) from lupus have declined since the 1980s as diagnosis and treatment have improved. However, the mortality rate for people of color continues to be higher than for Caucasians and has actually increased since the 1990s. A report from the National Institute of Arthritis and Musculoskeletal and Skin Diseases states that poverty is a more accurate gauge of mortality in lupus than ethnicity. So people with access to good medical care do better with lupus than those without access to good medical care.

CHAPTER TWO

THE IMMUNE SYSTEM

Inflammation underlies the symptoms of lupus. The immune system is the part of the body that, among other things, triggers inflammation to fight infections. A basic understanding of the immune system is therefore necessary to understand lupus.

You have probably played computer games. In many of them, you have to protect yourself from enemies, such as aliens, armies, or dark forces. Your tools might include weapons, magic spells, or special abilities such as invisibility or superstrength. You might be able to use several tools together to give yourself even better protection.

The immune system is similar to many computer games. Its function is to protect us from foreign invaders, called antigens. It has different parts that work together to provide strong protection.

White blood cells called macrophages are a first line of defense. They act as scouts. They recognize invaders and destroy them. They also send out chemicals to signal other cells for help. The more numerous the invaders, the more signals are sent out and the more help arrives. If the macrophages can't do the job themselves, cells called helper T cells (or T4 cells, or CD4 cells) get the message and sound the alarm. They signal cells called B cells to start producing antibodies. These are chemicals that stick to the invader and paralyze it until the macrophages can destroy it. (The combination of an invader and the attached antigens is called an antibody-antigen complex.) The antibodies produced by the B cells are specific to the invader. The helper T cells also signal killer T cells to go to the area of attack and destroy cells that the invader has entered. Like the B cells, the killer T cells are specific to the invader.

In a computer game, the area of battle can get messy. The same is true of the body. Think about what happens when you get a cut. The

March 8, 2010

From the Pages of USA TODAY

Inflammation and how it triggers illness

Researchers are beginning to understand the ways being overweight or obese contributes to inflammation that can trigger heart disease, diabetes and other ailments.

Until 10 or 15 years ago, doctors thought of fat as just a bunch of cells that stored energy.

In 1994, researchers at Rockefeller University in New York discovered that fat cells actually produce a hormone that controls hunger and fat burning.

In 2005, a group at Columbia University in New York showed that when rodents were fed a high fat diet or became obese, their fat tissues became inflamed.

Normally, inflammation is healthy, a part of the body's fight against infections. But when it happens in response to obesity, it can contribute to numerous ills.

The inflammation appears to happen because macrophages, white blood cells that attack and eat infection, congregate in fat tissue.

In lean people, only 5% of fat tissue is made up of macrophages; in the severely obese it can be more than 50%.

Why? One hypothesis is that higher concentrations of fat could trigger macrophages to go into inflammatory mode.

When that happens, they shift from being simple eaters of dead cells to killers of foreign invaders. They bring out chemical weaponry, including cytokines, substances that carry signals between cells and can be used to attack and destroy infections.

In San Francisco, researchers did genetic engineering to see if the problem was fat itself. They created macrophages that could store more fat, introducing them through bone marrow transplants.

This protected obese mice against the fat-induced inflammatory response, says Suneil Koliwad, endocrinologist and author on the paper.

Koliwad calls the research exciting because it gives them "the potential for a therapeutic target to examine" when it comes to the ravages of obesity-induced immune response.

—Elizabeth Weise

area around the injury swells and gets red. It may feel warm or hurt if you touch it. These are signs of inflammation. They show that the immune system is doing its job.

After the invader is destroyed, an "all clear" signal goes out. The B cells stop making antibodies. The macrophages clean up whatever dead invaders and damaged cells remain. The swelling, redness, and pain decrease.

This system of cells and chemicals in the blood and body fluids can protect the human body from bacteria, viruses, and parasites that cause illness. The system turns itself *up* during an attack. It turns itself back *down* after the attack.

What if you're playing your computer game and suddenly the weapons you're using to protect yourself turn on you instead of on your cyberspace enemies? You might think twice before you play that game again. But what if the immune system turns on the body it is supposed to be protecting? This is what happens in lupus.

The immune system is usually very good at telling the difference between the cells of the body it is protecting and invaders that might harm the body. But in lupus and other so-called autoimmune diseases (*auto* refers to self), the immune system fails to distinguish between *self* and *not self*. For reasons that are not well understood, the immune system begins to produce autoantibodies (literally, antibodies to self) that attack specific tissues of its own body, causing inflammation. The immune system still attacks not-self invaders (bacteria, viruses, and parasites), but it also treats parts of its own body as not self. Since these body parts are always present, the immune system turns up to respond to a perceived threat.

In lupus the immune system attacks connective tissue. This type of tissue is found throughout the body in the skin, in the blood vessels, and in all the organs. When the immune system attacks itself, antibody-antigen complexes form in the area of the attack. Medical researchers think this accumulation of antibody-antigen complexes causes lupus symptoms. In a properly working immune system, macrophages and other phagocytic white blood cells would eat these antibody-antigen complexes. But in lupus, this doesn't always happen. It may be that the immune system is overwhelmed by the quantity of antibody-antigen complexes. It may be that the macrophages aren't working as well as they should. Whatever the cause, the antibody-antigen complexes get into the bloodstream and spread throughout the body. They block tiny blood vessels and interrupt the flow of blood. This situation can cause damage throughout the body.

Common Immune System Disorders

Allergies: About one out of twenty people is allergic to something, such as pollen, pet dander, or dust. In an allergy, the immune system treats a harmless substance as something dangerous. It pours out antibodies and chemicals called histamines against this perceived threat. Itchiness, watery eyes, and a runny nose are all symptoms of this overreaction by the immune system.

Type 1 (juvenile) diabetes: This type of diabetes occurs when the immune system destroys cells in the pancreas that produce insulin. Insulin controls the amount of sugar in the blood and keeps it at just the right level. Like lupus, type 1 diabetes is an autoimmune disease.

AIDS: HIV (human immunodeficiency virus), the virus that causes AIDS (acquired immunodeficiency syndrome), attacks helper T cells. The virus uses these cells to make more viruses and then kills its helper T cell hosts. With fewer helper T cells to signal B cells and killer T cells to do their jobs, the immune system is less able to protect the body. Eventually most of the helper T cells are destroyed. Infections such as pneumocystis pneumonia can occur and cause death.

September 4, 2007

From the Pages of USA TODAY

Mysteries of immunity unravel; Science is on the trail of perplexing diseases

Just three months ago, Reagan Williams, 9, was dangerously sick with extremely high levels of sugar in her blood. Today she's back on her feet and enjoying her first days in fourth grade.

Last week, Kylynn Welsh, 18, was in critical condition on a ventilator in a New Jersey hospital, unable to breathe on her own because of swelling that closed her throat. On Sunday, she was released from the hospital and will soon be starting college.

These young people have very different illnesses with one thing in common: Their immune systems have gone awry.

The National Institutes of Health estimated in a 2005 report that 5% to 8% of Americans, up to 23.5 million, have one or more autoimmune diseases, which occur when the immune system launches an attack on healthy cells within its own body.

"Almost every autoimmune disease, with the exception of rheumatoid arthritis, seems to be going up," says immunologist Noel Rose, director of the Johns Hopkins Autoimmune Diseases Research Center.

But whether that's because of an increase in disease or better recognition of cases is not certain.

Scientists believe autoimmune diseases are caused by a genetic predisposition activated by some environmental exposure.

"We don't understand all the factors influencing the immune system, but there has been an explosion in interest," Paul Strumph says. Possibilities include exposure to new germs, a result of international travel and commerce, a deficiency in vitamin D, an excess of cleanliness that stunts immune system development, even obesity.

But he and others who specialize in immune disorders are optimistic. The development of huge public databases about human genetics and technologies that allow scientists to test thousands of samples in a day will lead to new drugs tailored to a person's genetic makeup, new ways to predict susceptibility to disease and possibly ways to prevent them.

—Anita Manning

AUTOIMMUNE DISORDERS AND LUPUS

Malfunctions of the immune system cause a multitude of conditions. Several of these disorders, such as Sjögren's syndrome, scleroderma, and rheumatoid arthritis (RA), occur more frequently in people with lupus than in the general population.

STACEY

Stacey was coping pretty well with her lupus. But recently she noticed that her eyes felt dry and itchy. At times, her mouth was so dry that it was hard to swallow. She recognized these as new symptoms, but they didn't really coincide with her lupus flares. She mentioned the symptoms to her doctor. After some testing, the doctor discovered that Stacey had another autoimmune disease, Sjögren's syndrome, in addition to lupus.

SJÖGREN'S SYNDROME

A syndrome is a group of symptoms that occur together. In Sjögren's syndrome, the immune system attacks the glands that provide moisture to body surfaces, such as the tear-producing glands and salivary glands. The inflammation reduces the amount of moisture on the eyes and in the mouth, causing symptoms such as dry eyes and dry mouth.

Like lupus, Sjögren's syndrome can be mild, moderate, or severe. There are periods of symptoms and periods of remission, a period during which the symptoms of a disease are reduced or disappear. In more serious forms of the disease, the immune system attacks moisture-producing glands of the kidney, liver, lungs, nervous system, and gastrointestinal system.

About half the people with Sjögren's syndrome have no other autoimmune disorders, but the other half do. This syndrome occurs in 5 to 15 percent of people with lupus.

SCLERODERMA

Scleroderma means "thick skin." There are two main types of this condition: local and systemic. In the local form, skin becomes inflamed, thickens, and becomes tight. The fingers, hands, arms, the face, and the feet may be affected. Over time the thickening may become so severe that the fingers and hands cannot be straightened or bent easily.

The systemic form of scleroderma may or may not affect the skin, but it always affects blood vessels or internal organs. It can affect the digestive system, interfering with a person's ability to swallow solid food. It can cause thickening of tissue in the lungs, making breathing difficult. The Lupus Foundation of America estimates that 4 percent of people with lupus also have some form of scleroderma.

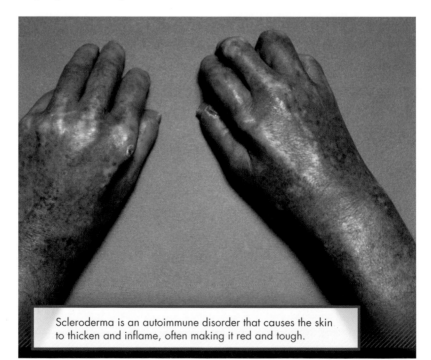

Scleroderma is an autoimmune disorder that causes the skin to thicken and inflame, often making it red and tough.

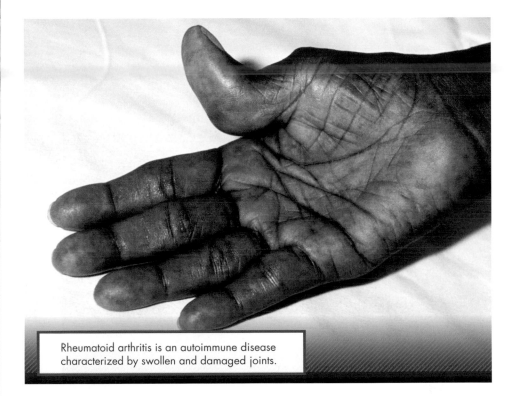

Rheumatoid arthritis is an autoimmune disease characterized by swollen and damaged joints.

RHEUMATOID ARTHRITIS

RA is an autoimmune disease that causes inflammation in the lining of the joints. It usually affects the hands and the feet.

Lupus often causes arthritis in the joints, but does not severely damage them. In RA the ends of bones at a joint are damaged, which causes deformity. The deformity can become so serious that people with RA have difficulty using their hands. If the feet are affected, walking becomes difficult.

CHAPTER THREE

DIAGNOSING LUPUS

JASMINE

Jasmine and her mother sat in the examination room at the doctor's office. This wasn't where Jasmine wanted to be. She didn't feel that bad. When Dr. Wilson came in, he took one look at her and said, "Oh." He pulled out his PDA (personal digital assistant) and started typing into it rapidly. The way he had said "Oh" had scared Jasmine. It sounded as if he had seen something really bad. Dr. Wilson turned his PDA so Jasmine could see the screen. It was almost like looking at herself in the toaster again. The girl in the picture had the same kind of rash. "Kiddo," he said, "I think you have lupus. Now here's what we need to do."

Jasmine was lucky. She had a well-informed doctor, and she exhibited the classic lupus rash. But many people are more difficult to diagnose. While many children with lupus have the butterfly rash, few adults have it. In adult cases, doctors have to consider other symptoms to reach a diagnosis. This process is made more difficult because many common symptoms of lupus, such as fatigue and joint pain, can occur with many illnesses or with no illness at all. On its website, the Lupus Foundation of America lists symptoms of lupus and how many people with lupus exhibit them:

- Achy joints (95 percent)
- Fever of more than 100°F, or 38°C (90 percent)
- Arthritis/swollen joints (90 percent)
- Prolonged or extreme fatigue (81 percent)
- Skin rashes (74 percent)

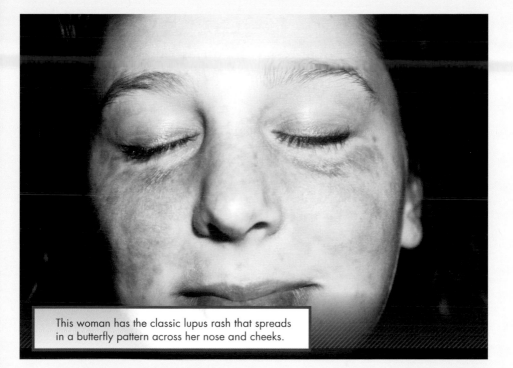

This woman has the classic lupus rash that spreads in a butterfly pattern across her nose and cheeks.

- Anemia (71 percent)
- Kidney involvement (50 percent)
- Pain in the chest on deep breathing (45 percent)
- Butterfly-shaped rash across the cheeks and nose (42 percent)
- Sun or light sensitivity (30 percent)
- Hair loss (27 percent)
- Abnormal blood-clotting problems (20 percent)
- Raynaud's phenomenon (17 percent)
- Seizures (15 percent)
- Mouth or nose ulcers (12 percent)

Many cases of lupus are misdiagnosed at first or shrugged off as growing pains or hypochondria (thinking you have a terrible disease when you're healthy). People with early symptoms often look healthy, but they know that something isn't right with their bodies. Not being able to find an answer to their health problem can make them feel frustrated and depressed. On average, people with lupus will see three different doctors over three to four years before they get an accurate diagnosis. Charles is a case in point.

CHARLES

Charles dressed for work and then went downstairs for breakfast. This was going to be a good day—he could feel it. His younger brother and sister had already had breakfast and were leaving for the school bus. His sister hugged him, and his brother gave him a high five as they rushed out the door. He watched them and smiled. Their father's death had been hard on them. He'd made the right decision to stay home and put off college until they graduated. He liked being the man of the family. He went into the kitchen. A magazine was on the table beside his plate of eggs and toast. He looked more closely. It was the prom issue of a girl's magazine. His sister must have left it. Then he heard his mother say, "There's an article in there I want you to read. Then I want you to take it with you to the doctor. You have a five o'clock appointment."

Charles waited impatiently in Dr. Gupta's office. He had been through this before and not just with Dr. Gupta. He had seen the sports doctor who worked with the high school athletes. He had gone to a doctor his girlfriend Denise recommended. The doctors all told him the same thing: get more rest and don't party so much. And now he had the stupid magazine article to show to the doctor. He shoved the magazine at Dr. Gupta without looking at him. The doctor looked at the cover of the magazine and said with a grin, "So you're looking for a prom dress?" Charles blushed to the roots of his hair and stammered, "The marked passage. Mom sent it." Dr. Gupta turned to the article titled

"Men Get Lupus, Too." After several minutes, the doctor looked at him, "Your mother might just be right. Let me get some more information from you. Then we'll do some blood tests."

Diagnosing lupus isn't as simple as a single test. It requires looking for clusters of symptoms and the results of blood tests. The American College of Rheumatology (ACR) has developed criteria, or standards, for diagnosing lupus.

Skin and mucous membranes:

- Butterfly rash on the face
- Discoid, or coin-shaped, rash of raised, scaly patches, which often occur on the neck, the face, and the scalp
- Photosensitivity, or sensitivity to light, causing a rash from exposure to sunlight or, less frequently, fluorescent lighting
- Sores in the nose, the mouth, or the throat that look like blisters and are usually painless

These skin lesions are the main symptom of discoid lupus.

Joints:

- Arthritis in two or more joints that includes swelling and tenderness. The hands and the wrists are commonly affected, but joints of the arms, feet, or legs also may be affected.

Internal organs:

- Chest pain caused by inflammation of the membranes lining the chest cavity around the lungs or membranes covering the heart
- Inflammation of membranes in the kidneys, causing protein that would normally be returned to the blood to be excreted in the urine
- Neurological (brain and nervous system) problems including headaches; confusion; faulty memory; seizures; and psychosis, a type of mental illness.

Blood tests:

- Reduced numbers of white blood cells (for fighting infection), platelets (for helping blood to clot), or red blood cells (a reduction of red blood cells known as anemia)
- Immune system problems as shown by abnormal test results
- False-positive tests (tests that say disease is present when it is not) for syphilis
- The presence of antinuclear antibody, a chemical the immune system produces that can attack the body

The most common blood test done to help determine if someone has lupus is for the presence of antinuclear antibodies (ANA). The test looks for autoantibodies to genetic materials found in the cell nucleus. About 95 percent of all people with lupus have a positive ANA test result. But there's a catch: many people without lupus also have a positive ANA test. For this reason, symptoms associated with lupus must be present for the ANA test to be useful in diagnosis.

The ACR recommends that at least four of these criteria are present for a lupus diagnosis. All four criteria need not be present at the same time. A thorough medical history is necessary to determine if any of the criteria have ever been present.

Additional Autoantibody Tests for Lupus

The anti-double-stranded DNA antibody (anti-dsDNA) test is positive in about half of people who have lupus and is rarely positive in people who do not have lupus. The amount of anti-dsDNA increases with severity of symptoms, so it can be one indicator of how the disease is progressing.

The anti-Sm test is also specific to lupus and can aid in diagnosis. The anti-Sm autoantibody attacks specific ribonucleoproteins in a cell nucleus and occurs in about 20 percent of people with lupus.

Antiphospholipid antibodies occur in about one-third of patients with lupus. They can lead to blood clots and stroke and can cause miscarriages. Their effects are called the antiphospholipid syndrome.

The anti-Ro and anti-La antibody tests check for other nuclear proteins. A positive result on either of these tests is of no significance to men with lupus, but women with these antibodies are at high risk for having a baby born with lupus. The anti-Ro antibody is present in 20 to 30 percent of women with lupus and is associated with rash in babies born with lupus. The anti-La antibody is much less common and seems to be linked to a heart condition in babies born with lupus.

Blood tests will provide an overview of the health of the body. The complete blood count (CBC) is a series of blood tests that counts the number of each kind of blood cell. Other tests measure levels of certain chemicals. The test results will tell the doctor if a person has an infection, anemia, or problems with blood clotting. They also will show how the body is handling sugar and whether the kidneys are operating properly. Additional information about kidney function comes from a urinalysis, or urine test.

CHARLES'S EXPERIENCE

In an ideal situation, each disease would have a set of symptoms that were totally different from those of every other disease. But, of course, medicine doesn't work like this. Researchers study a disease and try to find the group of symptoms and conditions that make it unique. They consider symptoms they can see; clues from patients' medical histories; the results of tests, such as blood and urine tests; and images, such as X-rays and computed tomography, or CT, scans. From all this information, they select the symptoms, the history, and the test results that when used together will be most helpful in making an accurate diagnosis. They disregard some symptoms. This isn't because the symptoms aren't real. They are. It's because certain symptoms don't help make the correct diagnosis.

In medicine, a favorite saying is "If you hear hoof beats, think horses, not zebras." What this means in practice is that doctors first look for obvious causes for symptoms, not rare or exotic ones. For example, if a person is sneezing and has a runny nose in winter, the doctor is likely to diagnose a cold. If a person has those same symptoms when tree and grass pollen counts are high, the doctor is likely to diagnose the condition as an allergy. In Charles's case, a young man with a strenuous job, family responsibilities, and a social life, it's no surprise that he feels tired. Add to this that he's a male. With this information, lupus as a possible cause for his fatigue is a zebra, not a horse. But in this case, Charles *is* a zebra.

The article Charles's mother sent to the doctor suggested a new way to view his fatigue. It changed how the doctor thought about Charles's medical history and suggested different questions to ask. Charles's medical records showed that he had had repeated episodes of pain and swelling in his hands, wrists, and knees during his teens. At the time, it hadn't seemed unusual. Charles was, after all, a serious athlete.

For some people, the first symptom of lupus is joint pain and swelling.

The information the doctor got from thinking about Charles's history in a new way and asking new questions helped him select which medical tests to do. The symptoms Charles has had and the results of the medical tests would give the doctor the necessary information for making an accurate diagnosis.

Diagnosing lupus continues to be a challenge. However, it has improved greatly over the past fifty years due to the development of the ACR criteria and of tests for the autoantibodies that are most often associated with this illness.

CHAPTER FOUR

TYPES OF LUPUS

Diagnosing lupus is even more difficult because there are four types of lupus recognized in the United States: SLE, discoid, drug-induced, and neonatal.

SYSTEMIC LUPUS ERYTHEMATOSUS

SLE is the most common type and represents about 70 percent of all lupus cases. Jasmine and Charles have this type of lupus. About half of SLE cases affect the skin and the joints and never progress farther. The other half of the cases also affect internal organs, especially the kidneys. The latter are the most severe lupus cases and may result in death.

DISCOID LUPUS

The name *discoid* refers to the raised coin-shaped or ringlike rash. Dermatologists (skin specialists) treat this kind of lupus.

DORA

Dora is probably in her early sixties, but she isn't going to tell anyone her real age. She's healthy and fit and, as she says, "she thinks and acts young." When she was younger, she was known for her big hats and long beautiful hair. She had a morning ritual of brushing her hair while she decided how she would wear it that day. When she was about forty years old, she started noticing a lot of hair coming out in her hairbrush. Later, she noticed a rash on her neck and scalp. The rash didn't itch or burn, but it left ring-shaped scars when it healed, and hair didn't grow back over the scars. Her doctor diagnosed her with lupus and prescribed medication for the rash. Over the years, she lost a lot of hair. The cream she used on the rash could be messy. Finally, she just shaved her head. She started wearing wigs and turned to high-collared blouses to hide the scars on her neck. She's still proud of her hair, but now her morning ritual includes having her granddaughters help her decide which wig to wear—the auburn one, the blonde one, or the black one.

Dora has discoid lupus, which represents about 10 percent of all lupus cases. In this form of lupus, only the skin is affected. It can be inconvenient and is sometimes disfiguring, especially when it affects the face. But this form of lupus is not life threatening.

British singer Seal was diagnosed with discoid lupus in his twenties. The scars on his face are a result of his battle with the disease.

Did the Author of *Little Women* Have Lupus?

Medical detectives from the University of Minnesota became curious about a portrait of Louisa May Alcott, the author of the classic novel *Little Women*. When they examined the portrait, it seemed to show a pale pink rash on her cheeks and nose in the shape of a butterfly. People thought that Alcott died of mercury poisoning from medicine she took. She had fragile health, and in her time (the mid-1800s), many medicines contained mercury. Researchers looked at her journals, where she often wrote of her personal health matters. She talked of fatigue, headaches, intestinal upsets, and nerve pain. These were not the symptoms of mercury poisoning. Was this lupus?

Dr. Ian Greaves and Dr. Norbert Hirschhorn think so. They published a paper describing why they think that lupus, rather than mercury poisoning, was the likely cause of her death.

This portrait of Louisa May Alcott shows her in her mid-twenties. She died in 1888. Researchers in 2007 proposed that the symptoms Alcott recorded in her many letters and journals pointed to lupus as the cause of her suffering and death.

DRUG-INDUCED LUPUS

Side effects are common with many medications. But it is less common for a medicine that is prescribed to treat one disease to actually cause another illness. Yet this is what appears to happen in drug-induced lupus. The lupus symptoms will generally go away after the person stops taking the medication that is at fault, usually within six months. Doctors treat lupus symptoms until the problem medicine is totally out of the body. Although many medicines can cause drug-induced lupus, only a few are responsible for most of the cases. Unlike SLE and discoid lupus, drug-induced lupus is not chronic. The symptoms will not return as long as the patient avoids the problem medication.

NATALIE

Natalie thought about what her grandmother had said about arthritis. Yes, she seemed to be too young to have it. But it probably wouldn't hurt

Common Medications
That Can Cause Drug-Induced Lupus

H

ydralazine: treats high blood pressure

Procainamide: treats irregular heart rhythms

Isoniazid (INH): treats tuberculosis or exposure to tuberculosis

Note that hydralazine and procainamide are older drugs. Newer drugs that have replaced them seem less likely to cause drug-induced lupus.

to see a specialist. She made an appointment with a rheumatologist. The doctor went over her medical history. Seeing that Natalie was taking the drug isoniazid (INH), he asked if she had tuberculosis (TB). Natalie explained that one of the members of her carpool had TB, so she and the other members of the carpool were taking INH preventively. When the doctor asked when the joint pain had started, she realized that it had been after she started taking the TB medicine. He explained that her symptoms might be lupus, and the INH might be the cause. He also suggested that she check with the doctor who prescribed the medication to see if it could be changed. He gave her a prescription to control her pain and swelling and ordered blood tests for her.

NEONATAL LUPUS

A newborn's immune system is not fully developed. This would leave the baby vulnerable to common infections. But something happens just before a woman gives birth that protects the baby. Some of her antibodies move into the baby's body and protect the baby while its own immune system is developing.

When a woman with lupus gives birth, she might pass antibodies associated with lupus to her baby. About 5 percent of women with lupus have babies born with neonatal lupus (a neonate is a newborn child).

Babies with neonatal lupus will have a rash and may have blood abnormalities. A small number will also have a condition called heart block, which causes irregularities in heartbeat. In very severe cases, treatment of heart block may require the implantation of a tiny pacemaker.

Like drug-induced lupus, neonatal lupus is not a chronic condition. As the baby grows, its immune system develops and the antibodies from the mother break down. As the mother's antibodies are broken down by the baby's body, the symptoms of neonatal lupus lessen and eventually disappear. A baby with neonatal lupus has only the symptoms of lupus. He or she does not have the underlying malfunction of the immune system that the mother has. When the baby's symptoms are gone, the baby no longer has lupus. However, babies born with neonatal lupus have about a 5 percent chance of developing lupus in the future.

The chronic forms of lupus, SLE and discoid lupus, account for 80 percent of all lupus cases. So the good news is that more than half of all chronic cases of lupus are not life threatening.

CHAPTER FIVE

LUPUS UNFOLDS

JASMINE

Jasmine ate a snack as she tried to sort out everything Dr. Wilson had told her. He told her that her immune system attacked her skin and that's why she had the rash. He also wanted her to see a different doctor and had made an appointment for her. She wasn't excited about going to see a pediatric lupus specialist next week, but she was glad that she could go to school and to band practice. "Just don't overdo it and stay out of the sun" he said. Dr. Wilson had smiled at her like he always did, but he seemed more serious than usual. He had given her mother a prescription, and Jasmine had already taken the first dose. She had cream for her rash too. Her mother sat down beside her, carrying a stack of library books about lupus. "What's our best offense?" her mother asked. Jasmine rolled her eyes but gave the expected answer, "A good defense." She reached for one of the books.

CHARLES

Charles had sulked at dinner. His brother and sister tried everything they could think of to make him laugh. Nothing worked. He knew it was unbecoming for a man his age to sulk. But he was Dunk, the jock, the cool dude, and Dr. Gupta thought he had a "girlie" disease. This was not cool. He could imagine the teasing he was in for. "Then it's your job to put them right," his mother had said. So now he was at his computer. His Internet search on lupus had produced more than thirteen million hits. He had a whole lot of reading to do.

Jasmine and Charles are embarking on an important step in their lives with lupus: they are learning about what is happening in their bodies and about the treatment they will receive. This step is important with any illness. But with lupus, it is especially important because the disease can be very different in different people. Being well informed makes a person with lupus a better partner in the treatment.

Lupus is a chronic disease, but for many people with SLE, the symptoms of lupus do not occur every day. They have periods of noticeable symptoms, called flares or flare-ups, and periods of remission, when the symptoms are mild or seem to disappear altogether. A remission period may last weeks, months, or even years. The flare itself may last only a few days, but the symptoms may get worse with each passing day.

People can take medications to bring about remission, but some people go into remission without medication. When a doctor takes a thorough medical history of a patient with lupus, it often becomes clear that the first symptoms of the disease occurred many years earlier. A woman in her twenties may recall that as a teenager she had "growing pains" or bouts of joint pain that weren't associated with strenuous activity. These may have been the first warnings that she had lupus.

In mild and moderate lupus, symptoms are mostly confined to the skin and the joints. They show up as rashes, joint pain and swelling, headaches, fever, fatigue, and sluggishness. Mental confusion and forgetfulness may also occur. It is not unusual for new symptoms to appear over time and for symptoms to become worse. Patients who experience pain in their finger joints might begin to have pain in their shoulders or knees. Patients with headaches might start having migraines. Patients who have been feeling tired might find that a simple act such as eating a meal is exhausting. These symptoms can be unbearable at times, but mild and moderate lupus are not life threatening.

In severe lupus, the disease affects the internal organs. The sac around the heart and membranes around the lungs can become inflamed, causing pericarditis and pleurisy. Inflammation in the nervous system can lead to seizures or a serious mental condition called psychosis. Inflammation of the filtering units of the kidneys can result in kidney failure.

Blood clots are another serious health risk for the roughly 25 percent of people with lupus who have antiphospholipid syndrome

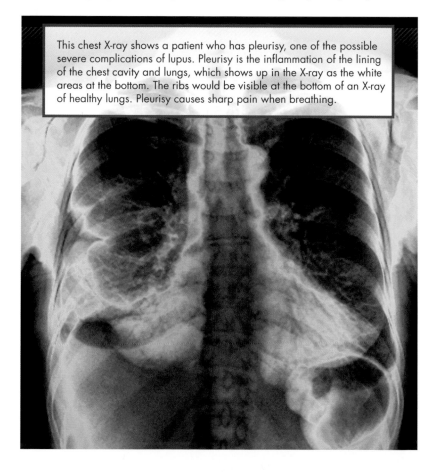

This chest X-ray shows a patient who has pleurisy, one of the possible severe complications of lupus. Pleurisy is the inflammation of the lining of the chest cavity and lungs, which shows up in the X-ray as the white areas at the bottom. The ribs would be visible at the bottom of an X-ray of healthy lungs. Pleurisy causes sharp pain when breathing.

(APS). Clots can form and travel to the brain, causing a stroke, or to the heart or lungs, causing blockages. Blood clots can also affect the ability of a woman with lupus to have a normal pregnancy.

THE LUPUS CYCLE

You can think of lupus as a cycle of a flare followed by remission. Sometimes a turn of the cycle is quite long. Patients with lupus might have an episode or a few episodes of a lupus symptom such as joint pain and then go into remission for years before this or other symptoms appear. The cycle can also be quite short or become shorter and shorter over time. Shortened cycles are often the experience that sends patients to doctor after doctor trying to find a diagnosis.

After lupus is diagnosed, one of the goals of treatment is to make the remission part of the cycle as long as possible using appropriate medications. But patients themselves sometimes can do things to reduce the likelihood of a flare. Avoiding situations that trigger photosensitivity is an example.

JENNY

Jenny gets terrible photosensitive rashes. Wherever light hits her skin, the skin turns red and scaly. It isn't just the sun. She can't use the fluorescent lights in her office because they affect her too. She dresses in slacks and long-sleeved turtlenecks and wears a wide-brimmed hat whenever she goes outside. She even tried wearing the hat in her office, but it got in her way. She also covers herself with sunscreen. One day, after what seemed like months of gloomy, overcast skies, the sun came out. It was February. The sun's rays were low in the sky so Jenny figured she'd be okay. She went outside without her hat to take a short walk in the sun. Within days she was having a lupus flare.

Lupus can cause extreme sun sensitivity. Lupus patients with this symptom have to take extra care to cover their skin when outside no matter the time of day or year.

Jenny was taking most of the right precautions. But not shading her face, even for her short walk, was enough to trigger a flare of her lupus symptoms. Other possible triggers include infections, medications, hormones, and stress. But no firm evidence supports any of these as triggers. Some people with lupus keep very detailed journals of how they feel, what they eat, what they do, how they sleep, and so on. Some of them find that this information gives them clues about when to expect a flare.

The Lupus Foundation of America has compiled the following list of things that might indicate that a flare is coming:

- Persistent fatigue out of proportion with what you would usually expect
- Persistent weakness
- Aching all over
- Fever, which may be slight to high
- Persistent loss of appetite
- Involuntary weight loss

- Increasing hair loss
- Recurring nosebleeds
- A sore on the roof of the mouth, which burns with spicy foods
- Unexplained skin rash anywhere on the body
- Hives
- Sores on the skin
- Painful joints
- Swollen joints
- Stiffness of the joints when waking up in the morning
- Chest pain that increases with breathing
- Shortness of breath
- Coughing up blood
- Persistent unusual headache
- Nausea or vomiting
- Recurring or persistent abdominal pain
- Persistent, increasing swelling of the feet and legs
- Puffy eyelids
- Blood in the urine

It is highly unlikely that a single person would experience all these signals, even over a lifetime with lupus. Rather, each person is more apt to have her or his own personal combination of a few of these signs that a flare is approaching. While flares can't be prevented with certainty, people with lupus can do some things to help reduce the frequency. First and most important, they should take medications as they are prescribed. Second is to keep all medical appointments, even when they're feeling well. Third is to call the doctor if they experience new symptoms or have any problems with medications. It's also a good idea to check with a lupus specialist if medications are prescribed by another doctor to prevent unwanted drug interactions. Finally, people with lupus should follow good

USA TODAY
News
SECTION A
NEWS.USATODAY.COM

March 31, 2011

From the Pages of USA TODAY

For many, 'D' in vitamin D means deficit
One-third aren't getting benefit for heart, bones

About one third of Americans are not getting enough vitamin D, a government report says.

The report, out Wednesday from the Centers for Disease Control and Prevention (CDC), parallels what many other studies have suggested in recent years: that a large chunk of the population is at risk for low vitamin D levels.

About two-thirds had sufficient levels, but about a third were in ranges suggesting risk of either inadequate or deficient levels, says report author Anne Looker, a research scientist with the CDC.

The results aren't surprising, says vitamin D researcher Marian Evatt, assistant professor of neurology at the VA Medical Center and Emory University in Atlanta.

"The known risk factors for having low vitamin D levels include getting older, being overweight and having chronic conditions. We're an aging, increasing-girth demographic," she says.

Numerous health problems have been linked to low vitamin D levels, including bone fractures, Parkinson's disease, diabetes and certain cardiovascular outcomes, cancers and autoimmune conditions, Evatt says.

Foods rich in vitamin D include fortified orange juice, cereals and milk, as well as salmon and eggs, says Holly Clegg, author of the Trim & Terrific cookbook series. Also, exposure to sunlight triggers the body's production of vitamin D, Evatt says.

Looker says the report shows the risk of vitamin D deficiency differs by age, sex, race and ethnicity.

"Deficiency was lower in people who were younger, male or non-Hispanic white, and in pregnant or lactating women," she says.

—Mary Brophy Marcus

health practices. This means avoiding the sun for the photosensitive, following a lupus specialist's advice on immunizations (injections that provide protection against certain diseases), getting enough sleep, eating sensibly, and not smoking.

KIDNEY DISEASE

Kidneys are the master chemists of the body. By way of hormones and other chemicals, they communicate with the brain and other organs to maintain the body's homeostasis (chemical balance). The kidneys filter the blood in an active, selective process to control its chemical composition. They remove urea (nitrogen waste) and other wastes from the blood and excrete them in urine. They control the pH (acid-base balance) of the blood, maintaining it around a neutral 7.4. They help maintain blood pressure and blood volume by removing water or returning it to the blood as needed. Every day all the blood in the body is filtered through the kidneys more than a hundred times.

Each kidney has millions of microscopic filtration units. Lupus inflammation damages these filtration units, causing the kidneys to malfunction. As kidney function decreases, other parts of the body are affected. Blood pressure can rise; fluids can accumulate in body tissues, especially the ankles and feet; and anemia and heart problems can develop.

HEART AND BLOOD VESSEL DISEASE

The third leading cause of death from lupus is disease of the heart and blood vessels. Atherosclerosis occurs when fatty deposits build up on the inside of blood vessels. The vessels become narrower, making it hard for blood to flow through them. In severe cases, blood vessels can become totally blocked. When vessels that provide blood to the heart become blocked, a heart attack can result.

Atherosclerosis is most common in older people, but women with lupus often develop what is called premature atherosclerosis. It is premature because the women are very young when they develop this condition. Doctors can monitor their patients' risk for atherosclerosis by using blood tests that are done regularly for lupus patients. If signs such as high cholesterol appear in the test results, medications can be prescribed to reduce this risk.

OVERLAPPING ILLNESSES

Most people with lupus find that managing their disease is quite a challenge. As many as one-third of all lupus patients have one or more additional disorders to manage along with lupus. You have already learned about three of these overlapping illnesses: Sjögren's syndrome, scleroderma, and RA. These three, like lupus, are autoimmune disorders. Two others, fibromyalgia and Raynaud's phenomenon, are also frequent companions to lupus.

FIBROMYALGIA

Like lupus, fibromyalgia is often misdiagnosed or not taken seriously. People with fibromyalgia seem to be extremely sensitive to pain. This condition results in fatigue, widespread stiffness, and intense muscle aches and tenderness. In addition to the pain and fatigue, which can be debilitating, common symptoms are headaches, difficulty sleeping, and mental cloudiness called fibro fog. To be diagnosed with fibromyalgia, a patient must experience pain at specific points on the body when pressure is applied.

No one knows what causes fibromyalgia, but it may be linked to physical trauma, such as an accident; viral infections; or medications. Until 2008 there were no specific medications for fibromyalgia. Doctors prescribe pain medication to relieve the pain and antidepressants to relax muscles. Since many people with fibromyalgia experience depression, antidepressants can serve a dual function. In 2008 the U.S. Food and Drug Administration approved a medication specifically for fibromyalgia pain. As many as 20 percent of lupus patients may have this condition.

RAYNAUD'S PHENOMENON

Raynaud's phenomenon is common among people with lupus. Doctors disagree as to whether Raynaud's phenomenon is an overlapping disease or just another symptom of lupus. This condition affects blood flow to the fingers and toes and, less frequently, the earlobes and tip of the nose. In response to cold, tiny blood vessels to these areas constrict and reduce the blood supply. The affected area shows signs similar to frostbite. It turns white, then blue, and finally, red. In the first two stages, the affected areas become cold, numb, and sometimes tingly. During the red stage, they can become painful, often with a burning sensation.

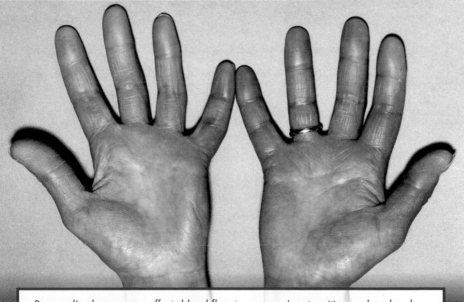

Raynaud's phenomenon affects blood flow to a person's extremities, such as hands, in response to cold. The person's hands can turn blue and tingle.

Keeping warm during cold weather is an obvious precaution. Covering the areas likely to be affected in layers is a good preventive measure, as is wearing a hat to prevent heat loss. But the symptoms don't occur just in response to weather. Holding a cold glass or a package of frozen food can also trigger symptoms. Symptoms can also result from vibration, such as that experienced when using electric tools, and from emotional stress.

An estimated 3 to 5 percent of people have Raynaud's phenomenon. But among people with lupus, this figure can be as high as 30 percent.

PREGNANCY AND LUPUS

Lupus is primarily found in women of reproductive age, which makes pregnancy a critical issue for these women. Angela's experience is not unusual. Many women with lupus have difficulty having children. Some give up, but others find the medical care that can allow them to give birth.

ANGELA

Angela and Ricardo love kids. Even before they married, they were planning for a large family, at least a basketball team. When Angela became pregnant, they were thrilled. They worked together to prepare the nursery. Ricardo's father, a cabinetmaker, built a beautiful cradle for his future grandchild. Then Angela had a miscarriage . . . and another one . . . and another. It was only after the third miscarriage that Angela learned she had lupus. An antibody test showed that she had antiphospholipid syndrome. It led to the blood clots that caused her miscarriages. She's pregnant again, but this time, a high-risk pregnancy specialist is following her closely. She's also taking medication to control blood clotting.

December 21, 2009

From the Pages of USA TODAY

Winter can be tough on the body

Winter can be hazardous to health—and may be especially tough on hearts, hips, hands and hides (your skin).

Heart attacks are more common in winter. When the body gets cold, blood vessels constrict. "If you already have plaque built up in your arteries, that constriction can decrease blood flow to the heart, leading to symptoms and a heart attack," says Jennifer Mieres, director of cardiology at the New York University School of Medicine.

Some studies suggest low levels of vitamin D, which the body produces in response to sunlight, might also play a role.

One study of 66,346 hip fractures in New York City found that fracture rates were highest in winter, especially on the coldest and windiest days.

"In cold weather, people venture out less," says Joseph Zuckerman, an orthopedic surgeon who helped conduct that study. "But when people do go out, there are greater risks, including ice patches."

Also possible: Winter inactivity weakens muscles, making falls more likely, indoors and outdoors. Low vitamin D levels, linked with weak muscles and brittle bones, might also play roles.

Cold hands are a common nuisance. But for 5% to 10% of people, hands and other extremities (feet, ears, nose, etc.) that overreact to cold are part of Raynaud's phenomenon. Stress or exposure to cold brings on attacks in which blood vessels constrict and skin changes color, often going from white to blue, then red, says Daniel Furst, a rheumatologist at the University of California Los Angeles. Pain and numbness can last minutes or hours.

For most people, the condition is harmless and best controlled by dressing warmly and avoiding cold. But about one-third have another underlying condition, such as lupus or scleroderma. So the symptoms are always worth mentioning to your doctor.

Take dry, heated indoor air, mix with dry, cold outdoor air, throw in harsh wind and long hot showers, and you have it: dry skin. So slather on lotion or skin cream, especially after washing your hands or showering. Keep your showers short and your soap mild. And try not to scratch: That can lead to infection.

—Kim Painter

Not all that long ago, women with lupus were discouraged from having children. Doctors feared that these women would have difficulties maintaining a pregnancy for nine months. Doctors also worried that pregnancy would make the lupus symptoms worse. But that thinking has changed over the last couple of decades.

But certain women with APS do have a high risk for miscarriage, and many women with lupus have premature babies. In fact, most pregnancies in women with lupus are considered to be high risk and require special medical care. But this doesn't mean that women with lupus should not become pregnant. It means they must have good prenatal care and work closely with a health-care team. This

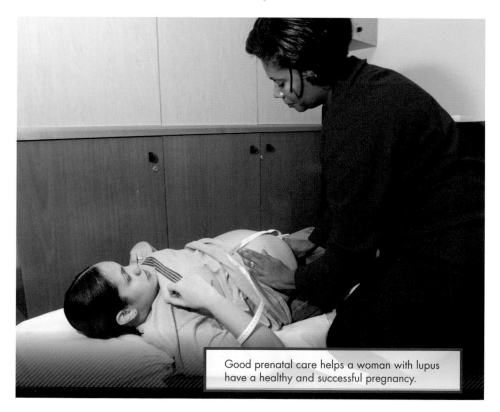

Good prenatal care helps a woman with lupus have a healthy and successful pregnancy.

may include tests to identify which autoantibodies are present in the blood. As with Angela, APS must be identified so it can be treated during prenatal care. A woman may have to stop taking certain lupus medications during pregnancy to protect the fetus. As a result, her symptoms might increase. But many women's symptoms do not get worse during pregnancy. Some women even report a lessening of symptoms, especially in late pregnancy.

CHAPTER SIX

TREATMENT

NATALIE

Natalie was relieved after she got a call from the rheumatologist. None of the tests indicated that she had lupus. The prescription he had given her was relieving her painful joints, and the nurse at the clinic had changed her TB medication. In a few more weeks, she'd be finished with the preventive TB treatment. Then she would see the rheumatologist again. Maybe, just maybe, these symptoms would all be gone in six months.

The doctor–patient relationship is of utmost importance in the treatment of lupus. The unique cluster of symptoms of the disease in each person requires an individualized treatment plan for each patient. Treatment works better when the patient pays attention to changes in symptoms and possible side effects of medication and reports these concerns to the doctor. The physician in turn builds trust by listening carefully and responding to the patient's questions. Lupus medications have serious side effects. Trust between the doctor and patient increases the likelihood that patients will follow their doctors' recommendations.

LUPUS MEDICATIONS

There are four groups of lupus medications: nonsteroidal anti-inflammatory drugs (NSAIDs), corticosteroids, antimalarials, and immosuppressive drugs. Doctors may prescribe them individually or together. A person might take one medication during the early stages of the illness and another, more potent medication later, if the disease progresses. Additional medications may be prescribed to treat the side effects of the lupus drugs. It can take time for the doctor and patient to find just the right medication and just the right dosage to treat the symptoms.

NONSTEROIDAL ANTI-INFLAMMATORY DRUGS

You probably know these medications as aspirin, ibuprofen, and naproxen. These over-the-counter drugs are commonly used to treat minor aches and pains. They are called anti-inflammatory drugs because they block chemicals produced by the immune system that cause swelling and pain. The rashes and joint pain of lupus are the result of inflammation, so these medications can be useful in mild lupus. A doctor can prescribe more potent NSAIDs.

Although NSAIDs can be quite useful in mild lupus, their side effects can be serious, especially after long-term use. They can irritate the stomach and intestines and cause ulcers and bleeding. Aspirin

What about Tylenol?

Tylenol is one of the most widely used over-the-counter medications. It is used to treat pain and fever. Its active ingredient, acetaminophen, is not an anti-inflammatory, so it is not very effective in relieving lupus symptoms. However, a woman with lupus may use it for aches and fever during pregnancy, when nonsteroidal anti-inflammatory drugs are avoided because of their side effects.

can reduce blood clotting. You may know older adults who take an aspirin each day to reduce the risk of blood clots that can lead to a heart attack or a stroke. But people with lupus don't take just one aspirin a day. They require larger, more frequent doses, especially when they have painful flares. But prolonged use of some NSAIDs can cause damage to the kidneys, the liver, and the heart.

Doctors should monitor patients' use of NSAIDs regularly to be sure that side effects are not serious. If the side effects become serious or if the NSAIDs fail to provide relief from lupus symptoms, other medications are available.

CORTICOSTEROIDS

When most people hear the word *steroids*, they think about drugs that many athletes use to bulk up their muscles. These are anabolic-androgenic steroids (or anabolic steroids). They are synthetic, or human-made, substances related to testosterone, the male hormone. Doctors use anabolic steroids to treat delayed puberty in males and wasting (severe muscle loss) that occurs after some types of surgery and in some chronic diseases. These drugs are illegal unless provided by prescription and taken under a doctor's supervision. If athletes take these steroids to increase muscle size, they take much larger doses than a doctor would prescribe. They also take the drugs without a prescription or a doctor's supervision.

Male and female hormones are steroids that the body makes naturally. Cholesterol, the waxy substance that can clog arteries and lead to heart disease, is also a steroid made by the body. The steroids used to treat lupus and other inflammatory conditions are synthetic versions of the corticosteroids made naturally by the body's adrenal glands, which sit on top of each kidney. The adrenal glands regulate how the body burns and uses food. They also play a role in the function of the immune system.

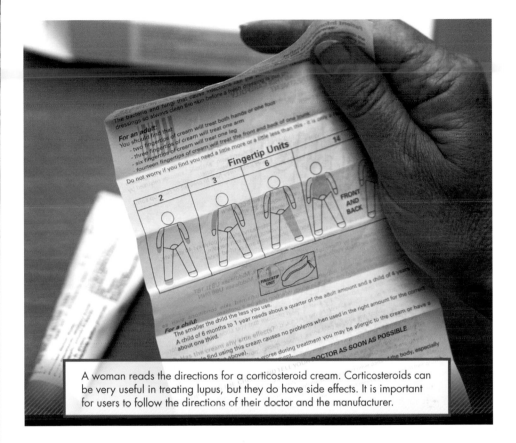

A woman reads the directions for a corticosteroid cream. Corticosteroids can be very useful in treating lupus, but they do have side effects. It is important for users to follow the directions of their doctor and the manufacturer.

Almost everyone with lupus will take corticosteroids at some time. Like NSAIDs, these drugs suppress inflammation, but they are much, much more powerful. If NSAIDs are a flyswatter, corticosteroids are a sledgehammer.

When there is a life-threatening crisis, such as kidney failure, doctors will administer high doses of corticosteroids intravenously. This treatment will quickly reduce inflammation and may save the patient's life. For more routine treatment, doctors prescribe lower doses in pill form or for rashes, in a cream or gel. The goal is to use the lowest dose of corticosteroids possible to control symptoms.

ERIC

When NSAIDs stopped relieving Eric's joint pain, his rheumatologist prescribed prednisone, a corticosteroid. It was like a miracle. He went back to playing racquetball twice a week and doing other things he had avoided because of the pain. He noticed that he enjoyed food again because the pain associated with holding a fork was gone. But even with all his physical activity, he was gaining weight. He also noticed that little things that hadn't bothered him before made him irritable and moody.

Eric is experiencing typical side effects of corticosteroids: weight gain and mood changes. Not everyone who takes corticosteroids will experience these particular side effects, but almost everyone will have some side effects from this medication, including the following:

- Increased appetite and weight gain
- Rearrangement of fat cells in the face, causing what is known as moon face
- Mood swings or irritability
- Sleep problems
- Nausea
- Acne
- Growth of facial hair or coarsening of facial hair
- Menstrual irregularity or lack of menstrual periods
- High blood pressure
- High blood sugar that can lead to diabetes
- Bone loss that can lead to osteoporosis
- Water retention
- Increased risk of infections
- Masking infections (hiding symptoms of infection due to lower activity of the immune system)
- Slow healing
- Bruising easily

Side effects vary from person to person. The dosage of the corticosteroids and the length of time a person takes them influence the side effects. High doses and long-term use are associated with the most serious side effects of these medications.

Increased risk of infections and the masking of infections are two especially worrisome side effects. Corticosteroids work by reducing inflammation—"turning down" the immune system, if you will. This is great for lupus symptoms because it reduces the autoimmune response. But it also makes the immune system less effective in fighting invading microorganisms. Latent infections, in which the microorganisms are in the body but are inactive, can come to life and cause disease.

TB is a common example of this type of infection. People on corticosteroids who have latent TB often take TB medications while they take corticosteroids to prevent active TB from developing. Keeping immunizations up to date is also recommended for people taking corticosteroids. This should always be done in consultation with a lupus specialist.

A person who takes corticosteroids might not know that they have an infection because the drugs cover, or "mask," the symptoms. Inflammation is one of the first signs of new infection. Corticosteroids hold down inflammation, so new infections may become serious before the person with lupus notices them. Infections are the second most frequent cause of death in people with lupus.

The chronic nature of lupus means that people with the disease might have to take corticosteroids for months or even years. To identify serious side effects early, doctors closely monitor patients. They regularly check blood pressure, blood sugar, blood calcium, and other factors. Blood tests can also show if a masked infection is present. Doctors might recommend calcium supplements to protect the bones, medications to control blood pressure or blood sugar, or antibiotics to treat infections. Diet and exercise can control other irregularities identified in the regular checks.

People who take oral corticosteroids should not stop taking them all at once. Suddenly stopping these medications can cause withdrawal symptoms such as joint and muscle pain, nausea, vomiting, fever, fatigue, and low blood pressure. Gradually reducing the dosage greatly reduces the withdrawal symptoms. In general, the longer a person is on corticosteroids, the longer the period required to reduce the dosage.

STAN

Stan had been on corticosteroids for twelve years when he developed osteoporosis. He didn't take the brittle bone risk too seriously until he was in a car accident. "I broke my hip and spine; the pain in my hip was awful," he recalls. "I had surgery, then rehab to get my muscles strong again. It was more than three months before I was comfortable walking again. I still have to wear a back brace for my spine. Sometimes I need to use a cane. Now I'm on blood thinner because I'm at risk for blood clots."

Long-term use of corticosteroids can cause osteoporosis, a disease in which bones become brittle and break easily. Bones of the wrist, the hip, and the spine are usually affected. The loss of bone in these areas occurs over time, making the bones weaker and weaker. Eventually fractures (breaks) can occur from even minor falls. Recovering from a fractured hip or spine is a demanding process. The corticosteroids that contributed to osteoporosis can also slow the healing process.

This side effect can be debilitating, but it can also be prevented. Calcium and vitamin D supplements can reduce bone loss. Doctors recommend regular weight-bearing exercise, such as walking, climbing stairs, and weight lifting. If these measures aren't enough, doctors may prescribe medication to promote bone growth.

CHARLES

Dr. Gupta had found a rheumatologist for Charles who specialized in treating lupus in men. Charles was surprised to discover that Dr. Harris was a woman. She explained that she had chosen the specialty because her older brother had died of lupus. He hadn't been properly diagnosed until he was very ill. This information made Charles feel comfortable with her. By the end of the appointment, he felt she would take good care of him. She had answered all his questions

Doctors recommend that people who take corticosteroids participate in a weight-bearing exercise such as weight lifting on a regular basis. This exercise can help counteract osteoporosis, one of the negative effects of corticosteroids.

and told him to call her if he had any new symptoms—even if they weren't on the list she had given him. She wrote a prescription for hydroxychloroquine and told him about possible side effects. She warned him to be patient. It would take at least six weeks before he would see any results. When he got home, Charles looked up the medication on the Internet. It was a malaria drug. What did malaria have to do with lupus?

ANTIMALARIALS

Antimalarials are a group of drugs used to prevent or treat malaria. Like Charles, you may be wondering what malaria drugs have to do with lupus. The explanation goes back to the late 1800s. At that time, there weren't a lot of medicines for any type of illness, so doctors tried whatever they had on hand to treat whatever illness their patients had. Quinine was one of the things they had. It had been used to treat malaria since the mid-1600s. Doctors noticed that lupus rashes cleared up when patients took quinine. This observation was a start, but the treatment did not spread widely. Then, during World War II (1939–1945), about four million U.S., British, and Canadian soldiers took a synthetic drug called Atabrine to prevent malaria. Many of these soldiers took Atabrine for several years. Atabrine worked to reduce malaria, but it had another effect. Soldiers with lupus or arthritis showed fewer symptoms. Research after World War II confirmed that antimalarial drugs were useful in treating lupus.

Antimalarial drugs have many advantages in the treatment of lupus. They are anti-inflammatory, they reduce cholesterol levels, they protect the skin from ultraviolet radiation, and they reduce the formation of blood clots. There is even evidence that they reduce the production of autoantibodies. Antimalarials are also effective at treating rashes and the pain and swelling of joints. They are the only lupus medication that treats fatigue. Recent research has shown that patients taking hydroxychloroquine are less likely to develop kidney disease.

Antimalarials work more slowly than NSAIDs and corticosteroids. They must be taken for six to twelve weeks before they begin to relieve lupus symptoms. It takes several months before they reach their peak effectiveness. Of course, there are side effects, but most are relatively minor when compared to those of corticosteroids. When a person first begins antimalarials, she or he may have gastrointestinal symptoms such as nausea, bloating, and diarrhea. Usually these symptoms go away as the body gets used to the medication or if the dosage is altered.

The most serious side effect occurs in the eyes and usually takes many years to develop. However, it is quite rare. In some people who take antimalarials, pigment (a coloring agent) is deposited on the

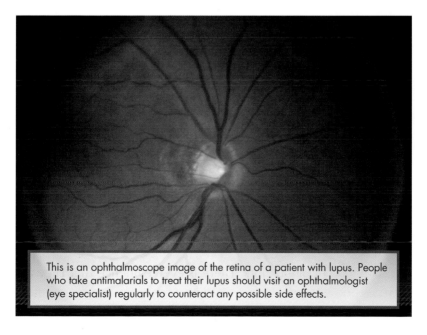

This is an ophthalmoscope image of the retina of a patient with lupus. People who take antimalarials to treat their lupus should visit an ophthalmologist (eye specialist) regularly to counteract any possible side effects.

retina, the membrane at the back of the eye that is responsible for vision. This is not immediately evident. Vision seems to be normal until a great deal of damage is already done. People who take anti-malarials are advised to see an ophthalmologist at least once a year. The ophthalmologist will do specific tests to see if there is any pigment buildup. If this occurs, the antimalarials are stopped. When the condition is caught early, the pigment usually breaks down and disappears.

Other vision problems can occur with antimalarials, including blurred vision and seeing halos, or rings, around lights. Patients with these symptoms are urged to wear good sunglasses, not only in sunlight but also around any high-intensity light source, including halogen lamps.

Although corticosteroids are more frequently used, some lupus specialists prefer to use antimalarials alone or with NSAIDs, as long as internal organs are not affected. The overall effectiveness of the antimalarials and the low occurrence of side effects are seen to outweigh the length of time it takes for them to work.

IMMUNOSUPPRESSIVE DRUGS

Immunosuppressive drugs do just what their name suggests: they depress the activity of the immune system. Drugs in this category were first developed to prevent the rejection of a transplanted organ. They are also used in chemotherapy to treat cancer. Immunosuppressive drugs work by slowing the formation of T cells and B cells, which results in a decline in the production of antibodies, including autoantibodies. These are very powerful drugs and must be used with great caution.

Immunosuppressive drugs are used in two major ways with lupus patients. The first is to treat life-threatening organ failure. The drug most commonly used for this is cyclophosphamide. Although it can be taken as a pill or an injection, in cases of organ failure, it is often given in pulse therapy. In this therapy, a patient receives a large dose of the drug intravenously. After a specific number of days or weeks, the patient gets another intravenous dose. This process is repeated for up to two years. Sometimes a corticosteroid and cyclophosphamide are used together. This therapy has been very successful in treating kidney failure caused by lupus.

The second way immunosuppressive drugs are used is with corticosteroids. Used this way, immunosuppressive drugs are referred to as steroid-sparing. The goal of this method of therapy is to reduce side effects for long-term users of corticosteroids. As you have seen in Eric's story, corticosteroids act very quickly to relieve lupus symptoms. Steroid-sparing medications work much more slowly and may take several weeks to several months to become fully effective. However, when steroid-sparing medications are used with corticosteroids, lower levels of corticosteroids will provide the same benefits and produce fewer or milder side effects. The dosages of the immunosuppressive drugs used for this purpose are much smaller than those used to treat organ failure.

Immunosuppressive drugs, regardless of their dosage, are powerhouse drugs with a range of side effects. The minor side effects include nausea, loss of appetite, and hair loss. Serious side effects include damage to the reproductive system, including infertility, and a small risk of certain cancers. Immunosuppressive drugs also affect the ability of the bone marrow to make new blood cells. This can lead to decreased red blood cells (anemia) and decreased white blood cells, which reduces the body's ability to fight infection.

Clearly there are serious drawbacks to using immunosuppressive drugs. But they can be very useful for people who need to be on corticosteroids for many years. They can save the lives of people with organ failure.

TREATING KIDNEY FAILURE

Lupus can be especially damaging to the kidneys. When corticosteroids and immunosuppressive drugs fail to control this damage, the kidneys cannot function properly. They will begin to shut down. Without further intervention, death will result.

DIALYSIS

Dialysis is the usual treatment for kidney failure. The patient's blood is run out of the body and through a filtering unit called an artificial kidney, which removes waste products. Once the machine cleans the blood, it returns it to the patient's body. This takes about four hours. People normally undergo dialysis treatment three times a week. Dialysis usually takes place at a hospital or a dialysis center.

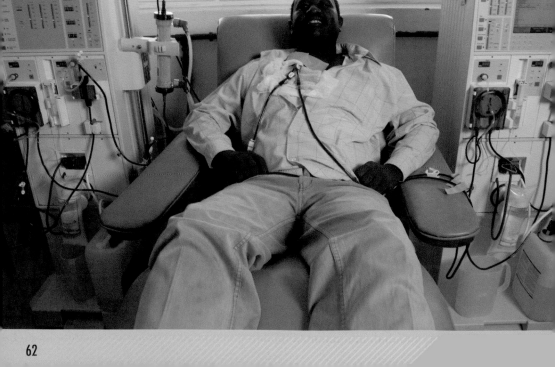

This man is receiving dialysis. His blood is removed through the tubes inserted in his chest, filtered in the artificial kidney machine, and sent back into his body.

How hemodialysis is used to treat kidney failure

For more than 35 years, dialysis has been the most common method for treating advanced kidney failure. The vast majority of patients are treated at dialysis centers, where their blood is pumped, a few ounces at a time, through a machine the size of a small refrigerator. A special filter removes harmful wastes, extra salts and fluids. The process helps control blood pressure and maintains a proper balance of chemicals such as potassium and sodium.

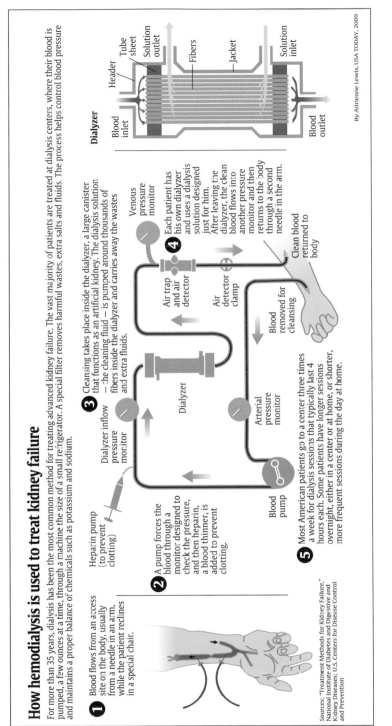

1 Blood flows from an access site on the body, usually from a needle in an arm, while the patient reclines in a special chair.

Heparin pump (to prevent clotting)

2 A pump forces the blood through a monitor designed to check the pressure, and then heparin, a blood thinner, is added to prevent clotting.

Blood pump

Arterial pressure monitor

Dialyzer

Dialyzer inflow pressure monitor

3 Cleansing takes place inside the dialyzer, a large canister that functions as an artificial kidney. The dialysis solution – the cleaning fluid – is pumped around thousands of fibers inside the dialyzer and carries away the wastes and extra fluids.

Venous pressure monitor

Air trap and air detector

Air detector clamp

4 Each patient has his own dialyzer and uses a dialysis solution designed just for him.
After leaving the dialyzer, the clean blood flows into another pressure monitor and then returns to the body through a second needle in the arm.

Blood removed for cleansing

Clean blood returned to body

5 Most American patients go to a center three times a week for dialysis sessions that typically last 4 hours each. Some patients have longer sessions overnight, either in a center or at home, or shorter, more frequent sessions during the day at home.

Dialyzer

Blood inlet

Header

Tube sheet

Solution outlet

Fibers

Jacket

Solution inlet

Blood outlet

By Adrienne Lewis, USA TODAY, 2009

Sources: "Treatment Methods for Kidney Failure," National Institute of Diabetes and Digestive and Kidney Diseases; U.S. Centers for Disease Control and Prevention

Dialysis can keep a patient alive and may improve health, but it takes a lot of time. There is also a risk of infection at the sites where the blood leaves the body and returns to it. Once a person with lupus-related kidney failure begins dialysis, she or he will need to remain on it for life or until a kidney transplant becomes available.

TRANSPLANTS

At one time, people with lupus were considered poor candidates for kidney transplants. Doctors thought that lupus would damage the new kidney. But according to the National Kidney Foundation, it is unusual for lupus to affect a transplanted kidney. People with lupus

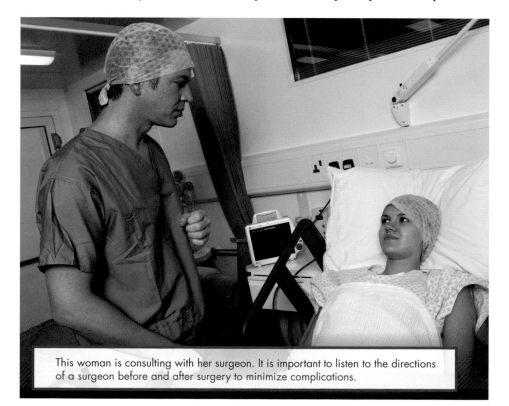

This woman is consulting with her surgeon. It is important to listen to the directions of a surgeon before and after surgery to minimize complications.

may even have an advantage. Some of the drugs they take to manage their lupus are the same or similar to drugs that are used to prevent the rejection of the transplant.

The National Kidney Foundation estimates that about 350,000 people in the United States have end-stage kidney failure. (This is from all causes, not just lupus.) Each year 67,000 of them will die.

According to the United Network for Organ Sharing, about 83,000 people were waiting for kidney

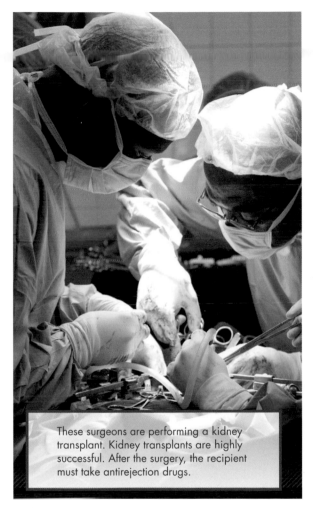

These surgeons are performing a kidney transplant. Kidney transplants are highly successful. After the surgery, the recipient must take antirejection drugs.

transplants at the beginning of 2009. During 2007, there were about 16,000 kidney transplants, far fewer than were needed.

Kidney transplantation is a successful medical procedure that has been done since 1970. Why, then, are so many people left in need? The answer is simple: there aren't enough donors. Deciding to donate an organ is a very personal choice. Many people only think about it when someone dear to them needs a transplant. Some people find the idea frightening. Others don't know much about it, so they never consider it.

Unlike a heart transplant, which can come only from someone who has died, a kidney transplant can come from either a living or dead donor. A live person can safely donate a kidney be-

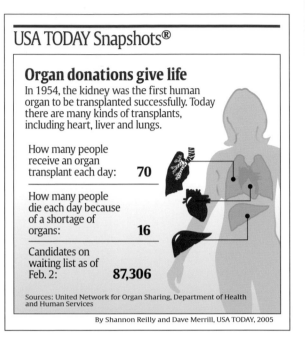

USA TODAY Snapshots®

Organ donations give life

In 1954, the kidney was the first human organ to be transplanted successfully. Today there are many kinds of transplants, including heart, liver and lungs.

How many people receive an organ transplant each day:	**70**
How many people die each day because of a shortage of organs:	**16**
Candidates on waiting list as of Feb. 2:	**87,306**

Sources: United Network for Organ Sharing, Department of Health and Human Services

By Shannon Reilly and Dave Merrill, USA TODAY, 2005

cause humans can live normally with a single healthy kidney. About one-third of donated kidneys come from live donors.

Many people have signed up to be organ donors. But often they do not discuss with their families their wish to be organ donors when they die. As a result, many potential organ donations are lost. But those who do successfully donate an organ, either in life or death, give a wonderful gift.

KEEPING IT IN PERSPECTIVE

Many things about lupus are frightening. But it is important to keep them in perspective. In half of all people with lupus, internal organs will not be affected. The other half, those whose disease will progress to the internal organs, usually progress to this condition slowly.

Regular doctor's appointments and regular blood tests can catch some problems when they have just started. This allows for early treatment, which may take the form of additional medications or changes in diet or other lifestyle factors. Some problems may develop suddenly, but they should not be cause for panic. Inflammation of the heart, lungs, and kidneys happens with many diseases, not just lupus. There are good treatments. People with these conditions who do well in treatment can live fairly normal lives for a long time.

CHAPTER SEVEN

CHILDREN AND ADOLESCENTS WITH LUPUS

GWEN

When Gwen told her mother that her urine was pink, her mother immediately called the doctor. Gwen had blood drawn at the doctor's office. She had to urinate in a cup so the doctor could analyze her urine. Dr. Wayne had looked at her rash. It was everywhere her bathing suit didn't cover. The rash had started after the swimming party for her eleventh birthday two weeks earlier. At the follow-up visit, Dr. Wayne had checked her over again. Her rash was fading, but it was still visible. She still had pink urine sometimes. The doctor and her mother were talking. Gwen could hear words she didn't understand, including kidney damage, immune system, lupus, *and* steroids. *She hoped Dr. Wayne could give her some medicine so she would feel better.*

Most of what we've said about lupus in the preceding chapters applies to children and adolescents as well as adults. But there are some differences. An estimated ten thousand children and adolescents in the United States have lupus. Children and adolescents have the same symptoms as adults, except that they are more likely than adults to have the butterfly rash. The diagnostic tests that adults take are the same ones used with children. However, when children are diagnosed, they tend to have more severe illness than when adults are diagnosed. Often, doctors miss the earliest symptoms of lupus in children because they are such common symptoms in childhood.

TREATING CHILDREN AND ADOLESCENTS WITH LUPUS

Gwen's case is typical for young adolescents diagnosed with severe lupus. The first diagnostic tests frequently reveal kidney damage. When this occurs, the child might get aggressive treatment with corticosteroids and immunosuppressive drugs to control the kidney damage as quickly as possible. For ongoing treatment, doctors use steroid-sparing therapy. When children are diagnosed, it means a very long course of therapy. Steroid-sparing therapy can reduce the risk of diabetes, high blood pressure, osteoporosis, and infertility.

New research may improve the treatment of kidney disease in children and adolescents with lupus. Doctors at Cincinnati Children's Hospital Center in Ohio have found a protein called neutrophil gelatinase–associated lipocalin (NGAL) in the urine of young lupus patients with kidney disease. Higher levels of NGAL indicate more severe disease. When treatment is successful, NGAL levels decrease. When treatment is unsuccessful, NGAL levels remain high or even increase. If further research confirms these results, NGAL levels may provide an easy way for doctors to monitor treatment and make quick changes in medications.

Children with lupus pose special treatment challenges. Young children may not understand what is happening to them. They may be frightened. The information that can reassure an adult may not be helpful to them. Older children and adolescents can understand more of the medical information about lupus, but they have other concerns. During adolescence appearance is becoming very important. The weight gain and round moon face that can result from taking corticosteroids can be upsetting and lead to thoughtless teasing by other kids. This is also a time of group identity and group activities. Participation in school clubs, field trips, athletic teams, and social events is very important. When a disease flare or episode of medication-related side effects occurs, important activities may

News
SECTION A
NEWS.USATODAY.COM
January 13, 2010

From the Pages of USA TODAY

True stories of heroic pets

Viola, a golden Labrador, belongs to the Children's Inn, a private, non-profit residence on the National Institutes of Health (NIH) campus where families whose chronically ill children are being treated at NIH can stay. Mars Inc. donated Vi to the inn in 2008 after she was retired as a Seeing Eye dog. The kids can spend time alone with Vi and attend special activities with her.

"Having a dog here helps the children relax, feel more at home, and makes their treatments more bearable," says Meredith Carlson Daly, media relations coordinator at the inn. "There have been many studies done showing how beneficial animal therapy can be. We see those benefits here every day."

Jak brings joy to the saddest and sickest of patients.

The Sphynx cat belongs to married medical professionals who understand the benefits of holistic healing. By also treating the mind and spirit, they think the body has a better chance of healing.

Terry and Sharron True registered Jak and two other Sphynx as therapy animals with the Delta Society, which has trained more than 10,000 animals across the world. The non-profit organization is

have to be curtailed. Concerned parents may limit their child's activities to protect her or him.

Young adolescents such as Gwen can encounter even more difficult problems. They may be out of school for long periods and may not be able to advance to the next grade with their classmates. When they are able to attend school, other students may be insensitive, because often kids with lupus don't look sick. They may also be shunned because their classmates do not understand the nature of the disease. In cases of severe, prolonged illness, a young person may lose connections to peers when this contact is important for social development.

founded on studies showing petting an animal can decrease patient anxiety, lower blood pressure, help ward off depression and allow healing to begin.

Jak helps out by making weekly rounds with the Trues at the J.W. Sommer Rehabilitation Unit in Muscle Shoals, Ala. Sharron True works as a registered nurse in the operating room at Muscle Shoals. Her husband is a family physician.

"When people are in a hospital, they can't see their own pets," Sharron says. "Jak will just curl up in their laps and stay there, making himself at home."

Only several hundred cats are registered with the Delta Society. Jak was the first Sphynx. Terry True says holding the velvet-like feline is like "holding a suede hot water bottle."

—*Janice Lloyd*

Viola visits the Children's Inn at the National Institutes of Health in December 2009. Viola is a golden Labrador that offers comfort to children going through medical crises.

TONI

Toni had been a cheerleader. She sang in the chorus and volunteered in the children's unit of the hospital. That was then. Now, at the age of fourteen, she feels as if her life is over. She can't do any of the things she used to love to do. She has this awful disease and has to take this awful medicine. She's always hungry. But when she eats, she wants to throw up. Every morning she wakes up with more zits. She has trouble sleeping and always feels tired. Dr. Evans told her it was the medication and when they got the dose right, the side effects wouldn't be so bad. Well, they've been trying to get the dose right for more than six months and she still feels lousy. She knew she'd feel better if only she could figure out how to skip her medicine.

Living with lupus can be especially frustrating for children and adolescents. At a time when they are finding and exploring their independence, lupus acts as a series of giant stop signs. STOP going outside without sunscreen. STOP hanging out late with your friends. STOP eating junk food. The first year is usually the worst as doctors and patients work out proper medications and their dosages. But it can take four to five years before the disease stabilizes. This is a long time for adolescents. Toni may sound a little melodramatic, but essentially she is right. Her life is not really over, but it has changed in dramatic ways. Often people with a new lupus diagnosis will deny they are sick or become angry. They may try bargaining, "I'll take my meds all week without being reminded if I can stay out late with friends on Friday night."

When adolescents are trying to work out what it means to have lupus, their behavior may be erratic. They may ignore their treatment when they are out of their parents' sight. This behavior is called medical noncompliance. In serious cases of medical noncompliance, people stop taking their medications altogether. Young people may ignore doctors' recommendations when side effects really bother them or when the medications become a symbol of the disease that limits their lives. The adolescent loses sight of the larger picture: that the medications, even with unpleasant side effects, help control the disease. The road to acceptance of lupus can be a rocky one.

It is important that adolescents be allowed to take responsibility for the treatment of their lupus. Parents should encourage them to speak directly with their doctors and keep asking questions. Doctors must explain why the medications and medical recommendations are important. Changing medications or dosage or even adding

A lupus diagnosis can be especially difficult to handle for an adolescent. Talking to a counselor can help a person come to terms with the changes in lifestyle a lupus diagnosis brings.

another medication can help with the bothersome side effects. Young patients may need additional coaching on why compliance is so important. A nurse, a social worker, or a school counselor might be able to help. If this help isn't enough, psychological counseling might help young lupus patients come to terms with their illness.

CHAPTER EIGHT

LIVING WITH LUPUS

CHARLES

" I knew it was a bad idea. I shouldn't have agreed to it, but I wanted to please Denise. She wanted us to go to a lupus support group together so she could understand better what I was going through. I had printed out articles from the Internet. But, no, it had to be a support group. It was awful! I was the only guy in the room. A lot of the women were around my age, and several were really cute. Denise was not happy. I don't want to go to a woman's support group, but it would be nice to have someone to talk to. Mom and Denise are good listeners, but for some things, it would be good to talk to another guy. I'm trying to do everything the doctor told me to do: I'm eating better, getting as much rest as I can, and exercising. But I'm still waiting for the medicine to kick in. I really want to quit being so tired. When I tried to find a lupus discussion online I found them—lots of them—but it was all women. I know I'm not the only guy on the planet who has this disease, so I started my own discussion group called 'Guys with Lupus.' It took more than a week to get a response, but I got this from some guy in Australia: 'Hiya, mate. R u 4 real? I'm Brian from down under, Oz. I've had this thing for 2 yrs now—can't even tell my sheila—she just thinks I'm lazy. If u r 4 real, talk 2 me!!!!' Do you believe it? Australia!"

Living with lupus can be a challenge for even the strongest, most resourceful person. Toughing it out alone is not a very useful strategy. One of the most important things a person with lupus can do is find a support group of people who understand. This may be the kind of group Denise and Charles attended. Hospitals and lupus support

Support groups can help people living with lupus overcome the loneliness a lupus diagnosis can bring. They allow people to discuss their disease with others who understand what they are going through.

organizations host these groups. For people who are uncomfortable attending a group in person, an online lupus discussion group might be the answer. These groups are also an alternative for people who live in areas with few lupus resources.

Lupus support groups provide help in a variety of ways. They can help people understand their disease. Books and articles are valuable sources of information, but they can't tell the whole story. Some things and kinds of understanding can be shared only by people who have had similar experiences. They can provide a sense of community and offer a place where participants don't have to explain themselves. Support groups can also assist with everyday concerns and help solve problems.

Life
SECTION D
LIFE.USATODAY.COM

April 8, 2010

From the Pages of USA TODAY

Loneliness casts a shadow over mind and body

Jody Schoger felt utterly alone, "curled up like a turtle" in her hospital bed, where she was fighting a life-threatening infection after breast cancer surgery.

"I remember never even opening the blinds, just hibernating," says Schoger.

Like many people with serious illness, Schoger found herself cut off from family, friends and the "real" world outside the hospital. Although many people would have been happy to help, she never thought to call them.

As her story suggests, the pain of loneliness is caused less by being alone than by feeling alone, says John Cacioppo, director of the University of Chicago's Center for Cognitive and Social Neuroscience.

Researchers are studying the causes and health effects of loneliness. Lonely people tend to have higher blood pressure and weaker immune systems. In lonely people, genes that promote inflammation are more active, while genes that reduce inflammation are less active, he says.

"Loneliness is a biological process that contributes to being better social members of our species," he says. "Think about what happens when you give a toddler a timeout. You basically make them feel lonely. Then they come back and are more likely to share, to be generous, to take the perspective of the other."

Schoger—who has been cancer-free for 12 years—says she sometimes finds support in unexpected ways.

"If any survivor posts something onto Twitter or Facebook that they're 'having a hard day,' I can bet you 10 to 1 that he or she is surrounded by good wishes by day's end," she says.

"Yet the survivor, the one who is ill, has to be willing to take that step. Once he or she does, the burden of illness and its perceived isolation fades away."

—Liz Szabo

DASHI

"I've never had trouble finding help when it was an emergency. When my car wouldn't start and I had a doctor's appointment, a neighbor gave me a lift. When I have a flare, other mothers in our carpool switch with me and pick up the kids. But sometimes I just have a bad day and need someone to watch the kids for a few hours while I rest. In my neighborhood, it's hard to find a babysitter on short notice, so I just have to tough it out. We talked about this problem in my lupus group and I'm not the only one who runs into it. One of the women is a high school teacher. She arranged for ten students to work when we need them. I keep the list on my refrigerator and call them several times a month. Sometimes it takes several calls to find someone who is available, but they have been such a great help."

Dashi's group solved a common problem of mothers with lupus—child care. There are many other everyday problems that lupus groups help with, such as sharing names of grocers and pharmacies that deliver or auto repair shops that provide loaner cars. These may seem like small things, but they can ease the burden of a person in the midst of a lupus flare. Support groups can also offer recommendations for those who are seeking a new doctor.

Support for the person with lupus isn't always from organized support groups. It can be from caring family members, friends, and neighbors who are willing to learn about the illness. It's important for anyone with lupus to have someone to talk with and someone who can help out when needed.

JASMINE

"Mom watches me like a hawk. She's really strict about when I go to bed. I know she's worried, but I keep telling her I'm okay. She wanted me to keep track of how I'm feeling, so she put a sheet of paper on

the kitchen wall. It has rows with questions and columns for the days of the month. We go through it in the morning during breakfast and again before bed when I have a snack. She told me I need to be totally honest with my answers, because we'll take it to my next doctor's appointment. I'm not a liar, but there are just some things I don't want to tell her. Like the day I forgot my sunscreen and how I don't always wear that dumb hat. I want kids at school to notice me because I'm good at music or something, not because I look weird. I get worried about my little brother Max sometimes. He knows I've been sick. He made fun of my rash. I think it's scaring him. He asked me if I was going to die. I told him no, but I don't know if he believes me. There are some good things about having lupus. Mom doesn't nag me about cleaning my room as much. Sometimes she lets me sleep late. But there are lots of not-so-good things. Every morning when we do the chart, Mom has me list the things to do that day. Then she has me number them beginning with the most important. She says I only have so much energy so I have to set priorities. The problem is that after I number all the things I HAVE to do, there isn't much room for what I WANT to do."

MANAGING TIME, MAKING CHOICES

Coping with lupus requires learning to live within the limits of a particular set of lupus symptoms. If flares are rare, this might be fairly easy. If they are frequent or if some symptoms continue even during remissions, it can be much more difficult. Flares often strike without warning, so it is hard to plan very far in advance. Many people with lupus learn to live one day at a time, accepting that how they feel when they wake up often determines what they will be able to do on that particular day. On a good day, they may be able to go to work or school as usual, but on a bad day, activities will have to be restricted. Some days will be so difficult that even simple activities such as getting dressed or eating will be painful and exhausting.

Jasmine's mother is teaching her a valuable skill for someone with lupus: how to prioritize and make choices. Most of us have more things we want to do than time to do them. Sometimes we stay up late to hang out with friends or work on a hobby and then cut our sleep time short. As long as we don't do it too often, we're okay. But this is never a good idea for someone with lupus, especially since it isn't unusual for people with lupus to have trouble sleeping, even when they are very tired. So learning how much they can do on a good day, a so-so day, and a day when they are having a flare is really important.

SOCIAL CONNECTIONS

For people with large, close-knit families, the loss of friends may be sad but manageable. For people without family nearby, the loss of friends can leave them lonely and isolated. Here again, lupus support groups can help.

PAM

"The first year after my diagnosis I was a mess. The NSAIDs weren't enough and we couldn't seem to find the right dose of steroids. The meds made me irritable and I snapped at everyone. My lab partner in biology class got tired of what she called my 'attitude' and quit working with me. I'd plan to go to a party or a movie and would have to cancel at the last minute because I was too tired. I kept thinking I could do more than I could. I lost a lot of friends that year. They tried to be understanding, but I guess that can last for only so long."

Pam's experience is quite common. Social ties have to be nurtured to stay healthy. Friends often have a pattern of doing something together on a regular basis. This could be a weekly sporting event at school or a monthly potluck dinner at church. When the person with lupus can no longer do these things, the social ties get frayed and often break.

Pam's lab partner is an example of a real problem faced by people with lupus. Often people with lupus don't look sick. They usually don't want to explain their medical condition to the people around them. Even when they try to explain, they may be seen as making excuses for bad behavior, such as irritability or not being able to do their share of the work in a team situation. Even caring people may become impatient with someone with lupus who is not able to meet commitments.

DEPRESSION

When a person with lupus has symptoms that are causing or are threatening major changes, sometimes depression occurs. It can happen shortly after diagnosis when treatment is being developed or when there are annoying symptoms even during remissions. It often occurs during crisis periods, when internal organs are involved and the outcome is uncertain. Depression can also occur when lupus results in social isolation.

MARGIE

"When I found out I had lupus, I was furious. I have this dream job as project director at a graphic design company. I head this great team of artists. I get to travel all over, working with our clients. When I go to someplace interesting, I schedule my travel so I can have a weekend to explore. I worked hard to get this job. Now I'm afraid I'll lose it. I'm exhausted, I have rashes, and worst of all for an artist my finger joints

are red and swollen and hurt like crazy. My doctor said I shouldn't travel for a few months while we run some more tests and get the medications worked out. I can still supervise my team, so I'm going to work, but I'm getting very depressed. I've started seeing a therapist. I hope it helps."

Margie feels as if she has lost control of her life to this unpredictable disease. She is afraid she will lose everything she has worked for. It doesn't matter that the things she fears may not happen. Her fears are real. They are probably affecting how she is living her life while she is waiting to learn more about her medical condition.

Margie made a good decision when she decided to see a therapist because depression should always be taken seriously. Treatment for depression includes psychotherapy or medication or both. Therapy gives Margie an opportunity to clarify her concerns about lupus and explore her options for coping with her illness in a safe environment. Getting therapy for depression may also help her improve her skills for coping with lupus.

EXERCISE

It may be surprising that doctors recommend exercise for people with lupus, but it can be quite beneficial. When joints are affected, moderate exercise helps keep them flexible. Regular exercise also reduces the stress that people with lupus often experience, and it promotes overall health. By strengthening the body, some people are even able to reduce the fatigue they experience.

ADDIE

"When my doctor told me to start exercising, I told her she was crazy. My knees were swollen, I had a fever, and I was already tired. 'Not a

marathon,' she said, 'just a slow walk around the block.' So I tried it. The first day I only got as far as the end of the block. The next day I got a little farther. At the end of the week I got all the way around the block. What surprised me was that I felt better. I wasn't quite as tired, and my knees were less swollen. A friend suggested I get a dog for company on my walks. I found this little 10-pound [5-kilogram] bit of fluff with white spots that I named Fang. Anyway, it seems to be working. Fang and I go out almost every day. On good days we can do a mile [1.6 km] or more. On bad days we go to the corner and back."

Many people who were physically active before their lupus was diagnosed find that they can continue their activities once they get their medications worked out. Often people with lupus hike, bike, and even play sports. For those who can no longer participate in such strenuous activities, regular moderate exercise is still important. For all people with lupus, moderate exercise can enhance not only their bodies but also their sense of well-being. It is important for them to "listen" to their bodies so the amount and intensity of their exercise is beneficial rather than harmful.

People can choose from many kinds of exercise. Addie and Fang find that walking works for them. This is often a good choice because it provides a good workout, requires no equipment other than a good pair of walking shoes, and can be done anywhere. Other people prefer to practice yoga and tai chi, which move the body in slow, fluid motions that gently stretch the muscles and keep the joints flexible. Swimming works best for some because the water helps support the body. Alternating between different exercises helps some people stick with exercise by reducing the boredom of doing the same activity day after day. Exercising with a friend or an exercise group can help some people stick to an exercise routine. Exercising with others has the added benefit of providing an opportunity for social interaction.

Pilates is another exercise that is a good choice for people with lupus. It focuses on core body strength and overall mobility, which can relieve the pressure on joints.

MANAGING STRESS

No one needs to be told that high stress levels are not good. Most people know from their own experience that stress can make their hearts race, their anxiety increase, and their stomachs churn. Stress can also raise blood pressure, increase appetite, cause weight gain, and raise cholesterol levels. None of these things is good for anyone and especially not for a person with lupus. Just having lupus is stressful. When setbacks occur such as new symptoms or medication problems, the stress is amplified.

Stress can be caused by dramatic events such as the death of a loved one, being the victim of violence, or being in an accident. But it can be caused by other things as well. Happy events such as going off to college, starting a job, planning a wedding, or having a baby can also trigger stress.

There are many different techniques for managing stress. Some people use recordings of soothing music or nature sounds, while others prefer tapes or CDs that guide them through relaxation exercises. Meditation and deep-breathing exercises can have a calming effect and reduce stress. Yoga and tai chi combine movement with stress reduction. They can be quite useful for people with lupus who are under stress and lack the energy for more strenuous exercise. Many people find one or more of these techniques useful in keeping stress at manageable levels. Other people find that pursuing a hobby or reading a good book is all they need to manage their stress.

Finding a way to relieve stress is especially important for people with lupus. Reading a book, meditating, or volunteering can help relieve stress.

FAMILIES

Most books and articles about lupus focus on the person who has the disease. They are intended to provide basic medical information to patients and those around them. They may talk about the need for support or the problems of stress or social isolation. But few books talk about the dramatic effects lupus can have on a family.

GREG

"I've loved baseball for as long as I can remember. I'm ten, so that's a pretty long time. Every summer Mom took me to practice and games. She always sat up behind the backstop so she could see me good, because I'm a pitcher. She'd wink at me when I got one in over the plate. That made me feel great. But it's been different this summer. I have to carpool with my teammates and Mom doesn't always get to the games. I know she's taking medicine and sleeping a lot, but she seems okay otherwise. I really wanted her to come to our last game. I was the starting pitcher. She promised she'd be there. But at the game I looked all over for her and she wasn't there. I struck out five batters and she wasn't there! When I got home she was fixing dinner like nothing happened. My chest got so tight I couldn't breathe. I yelled at her, 'I hate you!' and ran to my room. I didn't come out, even for dinner. The next day Mom met me at school. We went to see Mrs. Dennis, the school counselor. I was still mad. Mrs. Dennis had Mom tell me about this disease she has. Mom told me she gets really tired and she forgets things, important things. Then she was crying and telling me she was sorry and that she loved me. I felt really bad. I didn't know Mom was so sick. I just thought she didn't love me anymore."

Greg was devastated when his mother seemed to have lost interest in something she knew was important to him. The support and encouragement she had given him for years was gone. He didn't understand why.

Lupus and other serious illnesses can have a dramatic effect on families. The illnesses can change the way people within the family relate to one another. Sometimes serious illness strengthens a family, but frequently it tears the family apart. Often the person with lupus is a wife and a mother, the person every other family member depends on for everything from clean laundry and nourishing meals to morning hugs and good-night kisses. She is the glue that holds the family together, keeping things from falling apart. Too frequently, an ill parent will try to hide the illness from the children or downplay it as a way to protect them. But as we saw with Greg, this approach rarely works.

When the ill family member is a child, the strain on the family can be enormous, especially if there are other children. Frequent medical appointments, supervising medication and other forms of treatment, and just worrying about a sick child can consume every free moment the parents have. Other children in the family often feel neglected or unloved. They may begin to do poorly in school or get into trouble.

The problems, misunderstandings, confusion, and frustration that confront a family trying to cope with lupus rarely work themselves out. The best chance for a successful outcome is some type of professional counseling. Greg's mother did the right thing when she went to the school counselor with him. It provided a safe place for her to tell him how ill she was and for Greg to express his anger. Family therapy, couples' counseling, and counseling with a clergy member can let people explore how a serious disease in the family affects each one of them. In this setting, they can grieve what they have to give up and begin to come to terms with new responsibilities. Counseling can also provide an opportunity for the whole family to

Family therapy can help families dealing with a lupus diagnosis. It can provide a safe place for family members to express anger, fear, and loneliness and can help family members learn how to support one another.

plan how they will make adjustments to provide support for the ill family member.

JIM

"When Evie told me she had lupus, I was devastated. The first thing I thought of was one of our high school teachers who died of lupus. Evie read my thoughts and said, 'It's not like Mrs. Stanton. I'm not going to die.' Then I thought about what the disease was going to do to us and to her. Between her part-time job, driving the kids to all their activities, and a different committee meeting every night, she rarely stood still. But she had worked this all out before she gave me the news. She was giving up all the committees but keeping her job. When we told the kids about Evie's illness, we were prepared for their questions and reassured them the best we could. Then we worked on a plan with

the whole family. Getting the kids to where they needed to go was the biggest problem. But our son Tony is sixteen and has his driver's license. We decided to let him drive the girls to school and practice on a trial basis, until we saw how he handled it. We were pleased with how seriously he took his new responsibility and how his relationship with his sisters improved. The girls and I took over grocery shopping on Saturday morning, and all the kids have been pitching in whenever Evie needs help. We're spending more time as a family, usually hanging out around the kitchen table sharing our day. Evenings are the hardest time for Evie. It's when she hurts the most. This has become our time together. We do quiet things, like watching old movies and reading to one another. I know this is going to sound crazy, but for our family, Evie's lupus diagnosis has been a gift."

Family meals and other dedicated time can help family members support one another as they adjust to life with lupus.

Jim's story shows how a family can come together and make the compromises necessary to support a family member with lupus. It wasn't easy. Evie had to give up community activities she loved. But she was clear on her priorities: her family and her job. The children had to give up some of their free time to take on more responsibility to help their mother. Jim made the decision to be with her during her most difficult time of the day.

These stories show many of the difficulties that a person with lupus faces each and every day. Having strong social ties, whether through a support group, family, or friends, is important for the person attempting to overcome these difficulties. These ties are crucial for solving practical everyday problems such as child care, reducing social isolation and depression, and supporting good health practices and regular exercise.

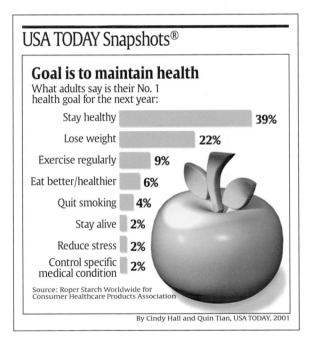

USA TODAY Snapshots®

Goal is to maintain health

What adults say is their No. 1 health goal for the next year:

Stay healthy	39%
Lose weight	22%
Exercise regularly	9%
Eat better/healthier	6%
Quit smoking	4%
Stay alive	2%
Reduce stress	2%
Control specific medical condition	2%

Source: Roper Starch Worldwide for Consumer Healthcare Products Association

By Cindy Hall and Quin Tian, USA TODAY, 2001

CHAPTER NINE

WHAT DOES THE FUTURE HOLD?

he visit to the pediatric lupus specialist had gone well. Dr. Danio was very impressed with the chart that Jasmine and her mother were keeping. "Jasmine, would you like to help doctors learn more about lupus?" he asked. She nodded and the doctor handed her a sheet of paper. It described a study for twelve- to eighteen-year-old females with lupus. Its purpose was to identify factors in their lives that were related to changes in their blood tests. The participants would answer questions about their lupus symptoms, diet, exercise, and stress levels every day and keep a record. At the end of each week, they would have blood taken for tests. Jasmine wasn't thrilled with having blood tests each week, but the questions weren't that different from what she and her mother were already doing. Jasmine handed the sheet to her mother. "I'd like to do this, Mom. What do you think?"

When we think about the future of any disease, often the first things we think of are research for better treatments and maybe even a cure. These are important, but other kinds of research can help improve the lives of people with lupus and other autoimmune diseases. Research into how the immune system operates and which genes are involved in lupus can improve our understanding of this disease. Development of better diagnostic tools can help identify lupus earlier and with greater accuracy. Identification of the triggers for flares might make remissions longer. Studies on how families react when one member has lupus can improve the coping skills of families. And, of course, research into treatments and the development of effective medications with fewer side effects can improve life for lupus patients.

From a scientist's perspective, figuring out lupus is a lot like working a jigsaw puzzle but with a big difference. When you work a jigsaw puzzle, you can see what it will look like when it is completed by looking at the box top. You also know how many pieces are in it and how large it will be. Scientists working on the puzzle that is lupus don't know what the final picture will be, how many pieces it will have, or how large it will be. In fact, it is their research that creates the pieces that make up the puzzle. Scientists have assembled small sections of the puzzle. One such section is about the immune system. Another is about medications that work to treat lupus. But even these sections are incomplete. Researchers have much more to learn about the immune system and treatments.

The study that Jasmine is considering will provide basic information about the relationship between lifestyle, lupus symptoms, and the blood. A lot of lupus research depends on the willingness of people like Jasmine and sometimes their families to participate. Lupus specialists like Jasmine's doctor may know about studies that are recruiting participants. Organizations such as the Lupus Foundation of America (www.lupus.org), the U.S. National Institutes of Health's Clinical Trials Department, and Lupus Together provide information about research projects that are looking for participants and links to research websites. These sites describe the purpose of the research, the type of participants they are seeking, and what will be expected from participants. People participate in studies for many reasons. They may wish to learn more about their disease, get state-of-the-art medical care, or make a contribution to medical research. Clinical trials that test new medications provide opportunities for excellent treatment at no additional cost to participants.

Some of the research discussed in this chapter will lead to advances in lupus care, but some of it will lead to dead ends, because that is the nature of research. But all of this research will lead to a greater understanding of lupus.

AREAS OF RESEARCH

The Lupus Genetics Study is an ongoing project at the University of Oklahoma that started in 1993. Its purpose is to identify genes involved in lupus. The researchers recruit families that have one or more members with lupus. These families live in the United States, Canada, the Virgin Islands, and Puerto Rico. All family members provide blood samples to be used for genetic analysis. Family members with lupus also provide complete medical records. One of the Lupus Genetic Study projects is the Lupus Family Registry and Repository, which includes more than fourteen hundred families. This project does genetic studies to find out how lupus affects different ethnic groups. It also shares the information and materials it collects with other researchers to do the following:

- Identify genes involved in the development of lupus and determine what they do
- Study autoantibodies
- Develop better treatments
- Look for a cure or way to prevent lupus

The ideal family for this type of research consists of three generations: the person with lupus, her or his parents and grandparents, and at least one sibling. Having a second family member with lupus adds information to the research. The research looks for patterns of genes that are different between those with lupus and those without. The project has not made any major breakthroughs so far, but small strides are being made.

Another group that is doing long-term research on the genetics of lupus is the International Consortium for Systemic Lupus Erythematosus Genetics (SLEGEN). This group includes researchers from around the world who are studying the genetic makeup of hundreds of people with SLE. Researchers compare these observations with the genetic makeup of people without lupus to identify genetic differences that will lead to better diagnosis and treatment of lupus.

The Department of Medicine at the University of California, Los Angeles, is doing research on lupus in males. Females have two X chromosomes (coiled chains of genetic material found in the cell nucleus). Males normally have one X chromosome and one Y chromosome. Males with an extra X chromosome (XXY males) tend to have lupus. Researchers are looking at the role of genes on the X chromosome in male lupus. This doesn't mean that all men with lupus have an extra X chromosome.

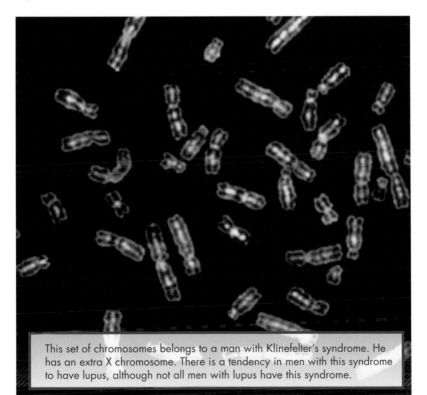

This set of chromosomes belongs to a man with Klinefelter's syndrome. He has an extra X chromosome. There is a tendency in men with this syndrome to have lupus, although not all men with lupus have this syndrome.

TESTS TO MONITOR LUPUS

When we talked about the immune system, we pointed out that it is turned on and turned off as needed to fight foreign invaders. Specific proteins provide the signals to control the immune response. Some children with active lupus lack a protein called PD-L1. It is necessary to turn the immune response off. When these children take medication, PD-L1 is formed again. Researchers at Seattle Children's Hospital are trying to develop an easy-to-do test that will determine the presence or absence of PD-L1.

EFFECTS OF HORMONES ON LUPUS

When we examined possible factors that cause lupus, one of those factors was female hormones. The Center for Rheumatic Disease and the Center for Allergy and Immunology in Kansas City, Missouri, is doing a three-year study of women aged eighteen to fifty to see how their T cells interact with estrogen, a female hormone. The study looks for differences between women with lupus and women without and tries to identify any genetic factors that are involved.

A concern about lupus in girls is that many require treatment with immunosuppressive drugs, which can affect their ovaries. This can lead to lowered fertility or even infertility when the girls become adults. Doctors at Cincinnati Children's Hospital Medical Center are studying the hormonal drug triptorelin to see if it will protect the ovaries from the medications used in lupus treatment.

LUPUS AND ORGAN SYSTEMS

Scientists at Northwestern University's Feinberg School of Medicine in Chicago are examining how lupus affects body systems. One study is following women with and without lupus to determine whether lupus plays a role in the development of osteoporosis. Another study

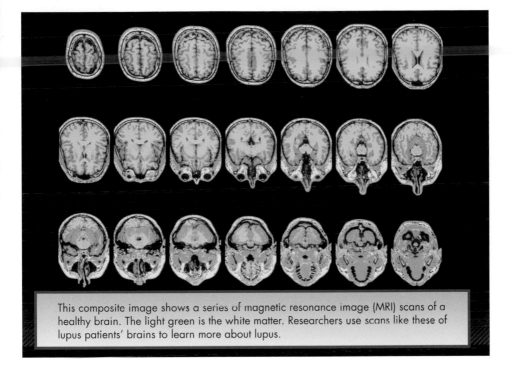

This composite image shows a series of magnetic resonance image (MRI) scans of a healthy brain. The light green is the white matter. Researchers use scans like these of lupus patients' brains to learn more about lupus.

will use images of the hearts and blood vessels of women with and without lupus to identify ways to detect heart and blood vessel disease caused by lupus.

A study conducted by the Division of Pediatric Rheumatology at Baylor College of Medicine in Houston, Texas, plans to study the brains of children with lupus. Researchers will look at changes in the white matter of the brain using magnetic resonance imaging. They want to see how these changes are related to severity of lupus, the amount of inflammation, and intelligence tests.

LUPUS AND THE IMMUNE SYSTEM

B cells of the immune system produce the autoantibodies that cause lupus. Some people with lupus, especially those with severe lupus, have abnormal B cells. A study by the Department of Microbiology and Immunology at the University of North Carolina at Chapel Hill is looking at the kinds of autoantibodies made by abnormal B cells. This research may lead to new ways to treat lupus.

At Yale University School of Medicine in New Haven, Connecticut, scientists are studying APS, which results in miscarriages and high-risk pregnancies in women with lupus. They are trying to learn how the antiphospholipid antibodies affect the function and survival of key cells in the placenta. This research might lead to new ways to diagnose and treat APS.

TREATMENT DEVELOPMENTS

For more than fifty years, there were no new drugs for lupus. Then, in March 2011, the U.S. Food and Drug Administration approved Benlysta, an injectable drug designed to treat flare-ups and pain caused by lupus. Benlysta is not effective against the deadliest forms of lupus and does not work for all patients. Lupus drugs currently in development include a new medication to treat kidney disease, a lupus medication that reduces symptoms by modifying the action of helper T cells, and a moisturizing cream for discoid lupus when steroid creams are no longer effective.

Researchers are also discovering new uses for existing drugs. Doctors at the University of Oklahoma Health Sciences Center identified 130 members of the U.S. military who developed SLE. Of these, twenty-six had received Plaquenil, an antimalarial drug, at about the time they had their first lupus symptoms. On average, these twenty-six patients progressed to ACR-defined lupus in a little over a year. The other 104 patients progressed in about three and a half months. This data suggest further study to see if antimalarials can slow the progression of lupus.

A research project at the Medical University of South Carolina is investigating a common vitamin that recently has been found to play a role in the health of the immune system. Scientists are studying the safety and dosage of vitamin D given to African Americans with lupus. Their long-term goal is to determine whether vitamin D therapy could be used to prevent or treat lupus.

STEM CELL THERAPY

Stem cells are in the news as a potential therapy for many serious, untreatable diseases. Stem cells are cells in the body that have the ability to develop into different types of cells. For example, stem cells in bone marrow can develop into any type of blood cell, including the T and B cells that malfunction in lupus.

The use of stem cell therapy for lupus has been studied for more than a decade. One procedure is to remove blood stem cells from a patient and grow them outside the body until there are large numbers of these cells. A very high dose of cyclophosphamide is given to the patient to destroy the patient's immune system. Then the stem cells are returned to the body. Medication stimulates the stem cells to produce new blood cells.

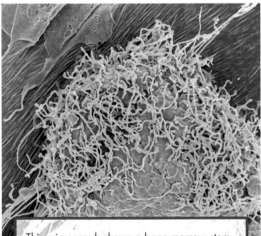

This micrograph shows a bone marrow stem cell. Bone marrow makes different blood cells and bone cells. Scientists are investigating if stem cells can be used to treat lupus.

USA TODAY
Life
SECTION D
LIFE.USATODAY.COM

February 24, 2010

From the Pages of USA TODAY

A bone marrow price tag?

Should people be paid to donate bone marrow?

About 20,000 bone marrow transplants are performed annually in the USA to treat blood disorders such as leukemia and anemia.

A lawsuit filed in federal court in California argues that too many patients are dying for want of a match. To encourage more prospective donors to sign up, the plaintiffs propose compensating bone marrow donors, a violation of the National Organ Transplant Act, which bans buying donor organs, including bone marrow.

Critics say financial incentives could lead people to cover up health problems or behaviors that would make them ineligible to donate bone marrow. They worry that paying donors will discourage altruistic people from signing up.

Because bone marrow produces immune system cells, finding a match is far trickier than with solid donor organs, says Jeffrey Chell, CEO of the National Marrow Donor Program's "Be the Match Registry." Even if all of the planet's nearly 7 billion people signed up to donate bone marrow, some patients, especially those of mixed race, still might not find a perfect match among them.

The Institute for Justice says 1,000 Americans die every year because a matching bone marrow donor can't be found. But Chell takes issue with that figure. "Many patients are referred too late for a transplant to be effective. Even delays caused by insurance denials can put a patient at high risk."

Plaintiff Doreen Flynn says paying bone marrow donors "didn't even cross my mind."

Three of Flynn's five children, Jordan, 11, and 5-year-old twins Jorja and Julia, will need bone marrow transplants for the treatment of Fanconi anemia, a rare inherited blood disorder.

"Jordan is very well aware of her disease," Flynn says. "She knows some of her friends passed away after transplants. She knows some survived transplants. And she's scared."

—*Rita Rubin*

This is an experimental procedure that is done only for people who are seriously ill with lupus and are not responding to the usual treatment. It requires a hospital stay while the immune system is re-forming and careful follow-up to prevent infection. Success is determined by the number of patients who go into long-term remission.

Doctors at Northwestern School of Medicine performed this type of stem cell procedure on forty-nine patients. About 84 percent of these patients survived for five years, with improvement in their symptoms. But this type of treatment is not risk-free. One patient in this group died as a result of the therapy.

The U.S. National Institutes of Health is conducting a small study on the use of stem cell therapy to treat lupus. Only fourteen patients, aged fifteen to forty years, are involved. The goal is to see if this therapy will result in remissions of at least two years.

Related research was carried out at Johns Hopkins University School of Medicine in Baltimore, Maryland, on a small number of

Stem cell researchers are exploring the use of the body's own stem cells to treat many diseases including lupus.

seriously ill lupus patients. As in the procedure that removes stem cells, the immune system was destroyed with cyclophosphamide. However, in this study, the doctors did not remove stem cells, allow them to multiply, and then replace them into the body. Instead, the body was allowed to rebuild its immune system with stem cells that remained in the body. After two and a half years, 30 percent of the patients were in long-term remission. Another 50 percent of the patients were responding well to medications that had not been effective before the procedure. It is too early to assess the long-term impact of stem cell therapy in lupus, but it is showing promise for specific groups of patients.

Residents of Kuala Lumpur, Malaysia, take to the streets with umbrellas to raise awareness of SLE in 2008. Events around the world are raising awareness of lupus and money to research new treatments.

The people who research a disease as elusive as lupus always hope for the breakthrough that will give them a better understanding. One of the studies described might be that breakthrough, or all of them may simply add additional pieces to the jigsaw puzzle of lupus. What the wide-ranging research does provide is hope. Hope for better understanding. Hope for better diagnosis. Hope for better treatment. There have been significant advances in lupus treatment since the mid-1900s, and we can expect more in the future.

GLOSSARY

antibodies: chemicals made by the immune system that bind with foreign invaders to reduce their harm to the body

antibody-antigen complex: the combination of a foreign invader (antigen) and attached antibodies that mark the invader for destruction by macrophages and other cells

antidepressant: a medication used to treat depression

anti-double-stranded DNA antibody: an antibody found in about half of people with lupus that can help in diagnosis

antigen: something that invades the body and has the potential to cause illness. Bacteria, viruses, and parasites are examples.

anti-La antibody: an autoantibody found in a small number of people with lupus. In women with lupus, it can cause heart block in their newborns.

antimalarials: medications originally developed to treat malaria that are effective in treating lupus cases that do not involve internal organs

antinuclear antibody (ANA): an antibody present in about 95 percent of people with lupus that is used in diagnosis

antiphospholipid antibody (APA): an antibody found in people with lupus that can lead to blood clots

antiphospholipid syndrome (APS): a group of symptoms that result from the presence of the antiphospholipid antibody. It can result in stroke and miscarriage.

anti-Ro antibody: an autoantibody found in a small number of people with lupus. In women with lupus, it can cause neonatal lupus in their babies.

anti-Sm antibody: an autoantibody that is specific to SLE and can be used in diagnosis

arthritis: joint inflammation that can include pain, swelling, redness, and tenderness

atherosclerosis: a disease in which fatty deposits narrow blood vessels

autoantibodies: chemicals made by the immune system that attack the body

autoimmune disease: a medical condition in which the immune system attacks its own body. Type 1 diabetes, rheumatoid arthritis, and lupus are examples.

B cells: cells of the immune system that produce antibodies

cardiologist: a doctor who specializes in treating conditions of the heart and blood vessels

chronic disease: an illness that lasts for a long time—sometimes a lifetime—or occurs repeatedly over time

complete blood count (CBC). a group of blood tests that provide information on blood cells. The CBC helps doctors monitor lupus.

corticosteroids: hormones produced in the adrenal glands. Doctors use synthetic versions of these hormones to treat moderate and severe lupus.

dialysis: a medical treatment for end-stage kidney disease in which the blood is filtered outside the body to remove waste and then is returned to the body

discoid lupus: a type of lupus that affects only the skin. It produces raised, coin-shaped (discoid) rashes that can result in scarring.

drug-induced lupus: a form of lupus in which the lupus symptoms are caused by a medication. The symptoms disappear soon after the medication is stopped.

fibromyalgia: an illness in which muscles throughout the body are painful and tender. Additional symptoms are fatigue and mental fogginess.

flare: a time when a person with lupus experiences a bout of symptoms

helper T cells: cells of the immune system that alert B cells to produce antibodies

hormone: a chemical produced by the body that acts to regulate processes within the body. Insulin, which regulates blood sugar, is an example.

immunosuppressive drugs: a group of powerful medications that "turn down" the immune system. Drugs in this group are used to treat cancer, some autoimmune diseases (such as lupus), and to prevent rejection of organ transplants.

inflammation: redness, swelling, and heat that result from the response of the immune system to an antigen

killer T cells: cells of the immune system that attack cells containing antigens

latent infection: an infection that is hidden and not active when the immune system functions normally but can become active if the immune system is suppressed

macrophage: a cell of the immune system that attacks and eats foreign invaders. It also acts as a garbage collector, cleaning up cell debris.

medical noncompliance: not following doctors' advice

neonatal lupus: a type of lupus that occurs in newborn babies whose mothers have lupus. It results from the mother's antibodies circulating in the baby's body and disappears after these antibodies break down.

nonsteroidal anti-inflammatory drugs (NSAIDs): a group of medications that reduce inflammation. Patients often use them to treat mild to moderate lupus symptoms of the joints.

osteoporosis: a disease in which the bones, especially the hips and spine, become brittle and break easily. It can be a side effect of long-term corticosteroid use.

pericarditis: inflammation of the membranes around the heart

phagocyte: any cell that ingests and destroys antigens

photosensitivity: a reaction to sunlight and other forms of light. In people with lupus, it causes rashes.

platelets: blood cells that help blood to clot

pleurisy: inflammation of the membranes around the lungs

psychosis: a mental condition that results in altered perceptions of reality that may result when lupus causes brain damage

pulse therapy: a treatment that administers high doses of medication directly into the vein at specific time intervals. It is used to treat serious organ damage in lupus.

Raynaud's phenomenon: a condition in which fingertips, toes, ears, and the tip of the nose become numb when exposed to cold

remission: a period during which symptoms of a disease lessen or temporarily disappear

rheumatoid arthritis (RA): an autoimmune disease that can cause permanent, crippling damage to the joints

rheumatologist: a doctor who specializes in the treatment of problems of the muscles and joints

scleroderma: an autoimmune disease that causes a thickening of the skin, especially of the fingers and hands

Sjögren's syndrome: an autoimmune disease that damages glands that produce moisture

stem cells: cells of the body capable of developing into many types of cells. Stem cells in bone marrow give rise to all the different types of blood cells.

stem cell therapy: a treatment in which stem cells are removed from a patient's blood, multiplied and, after the immune system is destroyed, returned to the body, where they can rebuild the immune system

steroid-sparing medications: drugs that can be used with corticosteroids so that smaller doses of the corticosteroids will produce the same medical effect. Doctors give these drugs to lupus patients to reduce the serious side effects of long-term corticosteroid use.

syndrome: a group of symptoms that occur together in a specific disease

systemic: referring to the whole body and its systems

systemic lupus erythematosus (SLE): an autoimmune disease that attacks connective tissue of the skin and body organs; usually called SLE, or lupus

transplant: transfer of a body organ or part of a body organ from one person to another. In lupus, kidney transplants can be used to treat end-stage kidney disease.

List of Acronyms

ANA: antinuclear antibodies

APA: antiphospholipid antibody

APS: antiphospholipid syndrome

CBC: complete blood count

NSAIDs: nonsteroidal anti-inflammatory drugs

RA: rheumatoid arthritis

SLE: systemic lupus erythematosus

RESOURCES

Alliance for Lupus Research
28 West 44th Street, Suite 501
New York, NY 10036
800-867-1743
http://www.lupusresearch.org
This organization funds lupus research, especially in the areas of genes involved in lupus and the biology of lupus.

Arthritis Foundation
P.O. Box 7669
Atlanta, GA 30357-0669
800-283-7800
http://www.arthritis.org
This organization provides useful information about arthritis, including arthritis associated with lupus.

Lupus Alliance of America
3871 Harlem Road
Buffalo, NY 14215
866-415-8787
http://www.lupusalliance.org
This organization provides information and advocacy on lupus-related issues. Its website provides basic lupus information, a lupus newsletter, and links to doctors who treat lupus.

Lupus Foundation of America
2000 L Street NW, Suite 710
Washington, DC 20036
202-349-1155
http://www.lupus.org
This site has a wealth of information on lupus basics, diagnosis, treatment, and coping. It also has features that help viewers locate lupus groups in their area and sources for lupus medications.

Lupus Research Institute
330 Seventh Avenue, Suite 1701
New York, NY 10001
212-812-9881
http://www.lupusresearchinstitute.org

This organization funds lupus research. Its website describes its funded projects and their research findings.

National Institute of Arthritis and Musculoskeletal and Skin Diseases Information Clearinghouse
National Institutes of Health
1 AMS Circle
Bethesda, MD 20892-3675
877-22-NIAMS (226-4267)
http://www.niams.nih.gov
This government organization funds research on lupus and related illnesses. Its website provides lupus fact sheets and information on research.

National Kidney Foundation
30 East 33rd Street
New York, NY 10016
800-622-9010
http://www.kidney.org
This website provides in-depth information about kidney disease and treatment.

S.L.E. Lupus Foundation
330 Seventh Avenue, Suite 1701
New York, NY 10001
212-685-4118
http://www.lupusny.org
Founded in 1970, this is one of the oldest lupus organizations. It has offices in New York City and Los Angeles. It provides support programs for people with lupus and runs educational programs to increase awareness of lupus among high-risk populations.

SELECTED BIBLIOGRAPHY

Blau, Sheldon Paul, and Dodi Schultz. *Living with Lupus: The Complete Guide*. 2nd ed. Cambridge, MA: Da Capo Press, 2004.

Pigache, Philippa. *Positive Options for Living with Lupus: Self-Help and Treatment*. London: Hunter House, 2006.

Sompayrac, Lauren. *How the Immune System Works*. 3rd ed. Malden, MA: Blackwell Publishing, 2008.

Wallace, Daniel J. *The Lupus Book: A Guide for Patients and Their Families*. 3rd ed. New York: Oxford University Press, 2005.

FURTHER READING AND WEBSITES

BOOKS

Bernatsky, Sasha, and Jean-Luc Snecal, eds. *Lupus: Everything You Need to Know*. Richmond Hill, ONT: Firefly Books, 2005. This book provides a balanced discussion of the medical and personal aspects of living with lupus.

DiGeronimo, Theresa Foy. *New Hope for People with Lupus: Your Friendly, Authoritive Guide to the Latest in Traditional and Complementary Solutions*. Roseville, CA: Prima Publishing, 2002. This practical guide is an easy-to-read introduction to lupus.

Edelson, Edward. *The Immune System*. New York: Chelsea House Publications, 1999. This book about the body's fundamental defense system provides a solid background for further study.

Hyde, Margaret O., and Elizabeth H. Forsyth, M.D. *Stress 101*. Minneapolis: Twenty-First Century Books, 2008. This book looks at the causes and consequences of stress, covering topics such as the health effects of stress, stresses specifically faced by teens, and practical advice on how to manage stress.

Lahita, Robert G., and Robert H. Phillips. *Lupus Q&A: Everything You Need to Know*. New York: Avery, 2004. A question-and-answer format that covers lupus basics.

Stefanakos, Victoria Scanlan. *Lupus: You Can Take Charge of It*. New York: Barnes and Noble, 2005. This book emphasizes ways to cope with the challenges of living with lupus.

WEBSITES

Could I Have Lupus?
http://www.couldihavelupus.gov/

This new website by the U.S. Department of Health and Human Services provides basic information about lupus, diaries of women with lupus, and forums for discussion.

WebMD
http://www.webmd.com

This general medical site provides good information on diseases of the immune system that often occur with lupus. It also explains tests clearly and describes what patients should do to prepare for specific tests and what to expect as side effects of testing.

YouTube

A search for *lupus* on YouTube will give public service announcements and information videos prepared by lupus organizations. This site also has video blogs by people living with lupus. To get started, try "Faces of Lupus" (http://youtube.com/watch?v=rC71qpgf2mc).

LERNER

SOURCE

Expand learning beyond the printed book. Download free, complementary educational resources for this book from our website, www.lerneresource.com.

INDEX

ABOUT THE AUTHOR

Karin Rhines has written educational materials on life science and biomedicine for more than thirty years. She has coauthored numerous science textbooks, written dozens of award-winning educational videos, and contributed to an eight-volume middle school encyclopedia on diseases. During her fourteen years with the Westchester County Department of Health in New York State, she directed programs in HIV/AIDS education and HIV testing.

PHOTO ACKNOWLEDGMENTS

The images in this book are used with the permission of: © Biophoto Associates/Photo Researchers, Inc., pp. 1, 3; © Jack Hollingsworth/Photodisc/Getty Images, p. 5; Courtesy of the National Library of Medicine, p. 6; © Scientifica/Visuals Unlimited, Inc., p. 9; AP Photo/David A. Cantor, p. 12; © SPL/Photo Researchers, Inc., p. 20; © Sue Ford/Photo Researchers, Inc., p. 21; © Dr. Ken Greer/Visuals Unlimited, Inc., p. 23; © Scott Camazine/Photo Researchers, Inc., p. 25; © Bambu Productions/Iconica/Getty Images, p. 29; Gregg DeGuire/Picture Group via AP Images, p. 31; © Time & Life Pictures/Mansell/Getty Images, p. 32; © Zephyr/Photo Researchers, Inc., p. 38; © Navarone/Dreamstime.com, p. 40; © BSIP/Photo Researchers, Inc., p. 45; © Eileen Brass/USA TODAY, p. 48; © Sheila Terry/Photo Researchers, Inc., p. 53; © Comstock Images/Getty Images, p. 57; © Science Source/Photo Researchers, Inc., p. 59; © Medicimage, LTD/Visuals Unlimited, Inc., pp. 62, 64, 99; © Laura Westlund/Independent Picture Service, p. 63; © Life in View/Photo Researchers, Inc., p. 65; © Darr Beiser/USA TODAY, p. 71; © iStockphoto.com/Chris Schmidt, p. 73; © Leonara Hamill/Stone/Getty Images, p. 75; © Robert Hanashiro/USA TODAY, p. 83; © Mcpics/Dreamstime.com, p. 84; © Bruce Ayres/Stone/Getty Images, p. 87; © Belinda Images/SuperStock, p. 88; © GJLP/Photo Researchers, Inc., p. 93; © Wellcome Department of Cognitive Neurology/Photo Researchers, Inc., p. 95; © Paul Gunning/Photo Researchers, Inc., p. 97; © Bazuki Muhammad/Reuters/CORBIS, p. 100.

Front cover: © Biophoto Associates/Photo Researchers, Inc.

Main body text set in USA TODAY Roman 10/15.